Building
Outdoor
Structures

Building
Outdoor
Structures

A Family Workshop Book
By Ed & Stevie Baldwin

CHILTON BOOK COMPANY
Radnor, Pennsylvania

684.1

Copyright © 1984 by The Family Workshop, Inc.
Published in Radnor, PA 19089 by Chilton Book Company
Library of Congress Catalog Card Number: 83-45384
ISBN: 0-8019-7503-4
Manufactured in the United States of America

Created by The Family Workshop, Inc.
Managing Editor: F. Van Huntley
Editorial Director: Janet Weberling
Editors: Mike McUsic, Rhonda Mulberry, Rob Dickerson, S.P. Bob
Art Director: Dale Crain
Illustration and Production: Wanda Young, Christopher Berg,
                                              Verna Stonecipher Fuller, Roberta Taff,
                                              Janice Harris Burstall
Typography: Deborah Gahm, Karl Lauritzen
Creative Director: April Bail
Workshop Director: D.J. Olin
Woodworkers: Charles Henley, Mike Garrett
Photography: Bill Welch
Project designs: Ed and Stevie Baldwin, D.J. Olin

1 2 3 4 5 6 7 8 9   2 1 0 9 8 7 6 5 4

This book is dedicated in loving memory of
Arthur T. and Anna Mae Baldwin

Preface

In producing this book we designed and built more structures than you will find between these covers. After much discussion, reexamination of the techniques involved, and an overall evaluation of the utility of the finished structures themselves, we settled on the final projects to be included. In some cases, the decision to include a specific structure seemed to be harder to make than in others. The hot tub, for instance, required an inordinate amount of testing and use before we could write it up for the book. It also was difficult to get our children out of the freestanding tree house so they could tell us whether they thought it was a worthwhile project. At any rate, we hope that you will find the projects you choose to build as attractive, useful, and easy to build as we do.

The book begins with a section on tips and techniques for buying and working with wood, for working with cement and brick, and for providing adequate drainage around the structure. We strongly recommend that you read this section thoroughly before beginning a project, as it provides basic information on materials, tools, and terminology. Coupled with the detailed instructions provided for each individual project, this information should make most of the structures manageable even for the novice woodworker. For the experienced woodworker, who knows, we might teach you a new trick or at least remind you of an old one!

Almost all of the project plans contain a list of required materials and provide step-by-step illustrations. For some of the larger projects, the gazebo for instance, our approach is somewhat more generalized. With projects of this size and scope, we felt that you might want or need to alter the size, shape, or configuration to your own specifications. Accordingly, for these few projects, we describe step-by-step techniques, allowing you to build the structure to your own liking. Most of the work can be done using common hand and/or hand-held power tools. In some cases, we did use shop tools (table saw, planer, etc.) to speed the process: Please remember, folks, we had to produce all projects in a very short time.

We would like to offer special thanks to a number of individuals and companies who provided materials, services, or tools for building the projects. The redwood stain that produces such a lasting and attractive finish was provided by the Watco-Dennis Corporation. The tools supplied by Shopsmith and Black & Decker performed like champions. A special note of appreciation is due Stephen Ward Smith who provided the luxurious greenery you see in many of the photos as well as his considerable expertise in landscaping, and to Rusty Barnett and Ernie Wilson who gave unstintingly of their time, patience, and good advice to make some of the projects a reality.

Contents

Tips & Techniques

Practically every woodworker with more than a few week's experience has his or her own favorite ways of performing the more common procedures involved in building things from wood. This is not an attempt to persuade you away from your own tried-and-true techniques, but rather is intended to provide some essential information concerning the materials, terms, and techniques that we used for the projects in this book. Some of the information may be old hat to you – some may be new – some you may disagree with. If there's one thing we know for certain about woodworking, it's that everyone approaches it a bit differently.

The information provided in this section is geared toward outdoor construction. The recommended adhesives and wood finishes, for instance, are not necessarily the same ones we would use for indoor furniture. Included here you'll find discussions of various types of lumber, preservatives and finishes, adhesives, fasteners, joints, and some miscellanea that will be helpful in using this book. At the end of the woodworking tips you'll find information on working with concrete, setting fence posts, footings and posts for decking, bricklaying for outdoor barbecues, building site drainage, and roofing. You may find several projects which refer back to the same individual section within Tips and Techniques. We suggest that you read the Tips & Techniques all the way through, or at least scan them, before you begin work on any project.

WOODWORKING TIPS

Selecting Wood

Different types of wood often have vastly different characteristics. This makes certain woods better for specific purposes than others. In addition, lumber is graded according to quality. We'll talk about types of wood for outdoor construction first, then we'll discuss the grading system.

Woods are divided into two general categories: hard and soft. Most hardwoods are much more difficult to cut and work with, but usually are more sturdy and long-lived than softwoods. Teak and oak are two hardwoods recommended for outdoor construction, with the latter being easier to come by as a general rule. Teak must be imported and is quite expensive. Softwoods are a lot easier to work with. The most commonly available are fir, redwood, hemlock, cedar, cypress, larch, spruce, and pine. Douglas is a particularly good fir; pine usually is available in both white (finer grain) and yellow (coarser grain).

Softwoods vary widely in their tendency to shrink, swell, and warp. Those least likely to do so are redwood, white pine, spruce, cedar, and cypress. Of these, cypress is more difficult to work with than the others and spruce is less decay resistant. Part of what makes a board more or less rot resistant is the portion of the tree from which it is cut. **Figure A** illustrates the difference between a heartwood board and one that is cut farther from the center of the tree. The more densely-packed annual rings near the center of the tree produce a highly rot resistant board, while boards cut from farther out may offer very little resistance, even when the stock is redwood or cedar. At the lumberyard, examine the ends of the boards carefully. The pattern of and distance between rings will tell you a lot about how long your outdoor furniture will last.

In the materials list for each project in this book we have specified the type of wood we used. We worked

Figure A

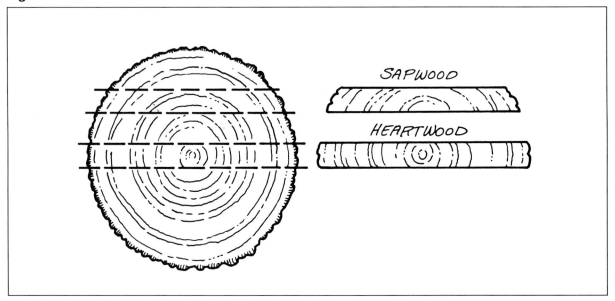

primarily with redwood, and sometimes oak. You may prefer to use other types of wood.

Lumber is graded, as we mentioned earlier. We have provided a rundown of the grading system for pine, which is also used for most other types of lumber. Keep firmly in mind that you need not use the highest grade of lumber for every (or any) project. As a matter of fact, for outdoor furniture you can get away with a much lower grade than what would be appropriate for fancy indoor furnishings. In most of our redwood projects, for example, we used #2 common construction grade lumber. If you are in doubt as to which grade to use for a specific project, talk it over with your lumber dealer. Show him the plans so he gets the whole picture.

#5 common – Full of knots, knotholes, and other headaches but the least expensive, this grade of lumber should be used only when structural strength is not required and when you intend to paint. It is prone to check (crack along the grain), and usually will not be as thoroughly seasoned or dried as the higher grades.

#4 common – This grade is low in cost and has lots of imperfections, but less so that #5. It is good for fences and other outdoor uses in which appearance is not crucial.

#3 common – Small knotholes are common and knots are sometimes easily dislodged while you work. This is a better grade than #4 or #5, but is still prone to check.

#2 common – This grade should be free of knotholes but still has its share of knots. It is often used for indoor flooring and paneling.

#1 common – This is the top quality of the regular board grades. It may have small knots and other insignificant imperfections but should have no knotholes and is a good choice for projects in which small defects are not important.

D select – This is the lowest quality of the better-grade boards.

C select – This grade may have a few small blemishes on one side, but should be almost perfect on the other. It is usually used for indoor work only, but may be used for outdoor furniture.

#1 and #2 clear – These are the best and most expensive grades. Spend the money if you wish to, but don't waste it! Use these grades only for the finest indoor and outdoor furniture.

In addition to being graded by quality, wood stock will be more or less "wet." Wetness refers to the amount of sap still left in the wood when you buy it.

Newly cut lumber is quite wet and must be air or kiln dried (seasoned) before it can be used. There is always some sap left, but it should be a very small amount. Wood that is not sufficiently dry will warp, crack, and shrink much more than dried wood. Unfortunately, there is no sure way to assess the amount of sap still left in the wood, even though the dealer may assure you it has been kiln dried. About the only hint we can give is to look at the end grain of each board (see **Figure A** again). Heartwood that is not sufficiently dry will become thinner as it loses moisture but is less likely to warp than sapwood.

When using lower grades of lumber, and consequently saving your bankroll, use your head as well. Buy a little extra so that you can eliminate the worst knots and cracks. You can repair the lumber to a certain extent by filling small cracks and gouges using exterior wood putty or a mixture of waterproof glue and sawdust. Warped boards sometimes can be weighted and straightened, but be aware that this takes time. Tap all knots to see which ones will fall out, and then glue them back in place. If a board is badly checked at the ends it's best to cut off the cracked portion, because exposure to the elements will worsen the cracks and perhaps even split the entire board. Minor checking should be filled as for cracks and gouges.

Preservatives and Finishes

Preservatives and finishes are especially important for projects that will be exposed to the elements for extended periods of time. You probably will be less than happy to see your hard- wrought (and dearly bought) projects rot in just a few years, so take heed and don't expect that using redwood or cypress will take care of all this for you.

The two major causes of wood deterioration are decay and insects. Some aromatic woods are naturally insect-resistant to a degree, but the less expensive grades are less resistant than the better grades, and you probably do not want to spend the money on top-grade lumber for all the projects you build. You'll be happy to know that this problem can be solved relatively easily — without purchasing pressurized vats in which to permeate the lumber with creosote!

Pentachlorophenol ("Penta") is the primary active ingredient in some of the most common modern wood preservatives. It is available in ready-to-use form, having been diluted in an oil base. You can pour it into a bucket and soak the ends of the boards, and you can also brush it onto the surfaces of the wood. It can be painted over.

Other effective preservatives include zinc and copper naphthenates. They are odorless and may be painted over, although the copper variety leaves a pale greenish stain that will show through translucent paint. Zinc naphthenate is colorless and can be used under clear finishes.

PLEASE NOTE that these preservatives are poisonous to both plant and animal life (that includes humans). Read the labels carefully and follow all precautions for storing and using them!!

For final finishing and sealing of outdoor projects, synthetic varnish is your best bet. You may wish to paint some of the projects you make, but if you use any of the more attractive woods it seems a shame to cover the natural grain and color. If you do paint be certain to select exterior paint. Varnish also must be an exterior variety, preferably a marine or boat varnish. Thin the varnish for the first coat, and then use it full-strength for the second.

Adhesive

We recommend both glue and fasteners (either nails, screws, or bolts) for all joints, unless you want to be able to disassemble the project for easy storage or transport. Aliphatic resin, which is the wood glue we normally use for indoor projects, will not do for outdoor furnishings. You'll need to find a waterproof glue, and be forewarned that the term is sometimes used loosely on product labels. We suggest that you use a marine glue or a two-part epoxy that must be mixed and used immediately. Waterproof glue may also be brushed on like paint to seal end grain and prohibit water absorption. As a general rule, all glued asemblies should be clamped, but not so tightly as to force out most of the glue. Thirty minutes is sufficient clamping time for most joints. Those that will be under a great deal of stress should be clamped overnight. Joints secured with power-driven screws need not be clamped at all.

Figure B

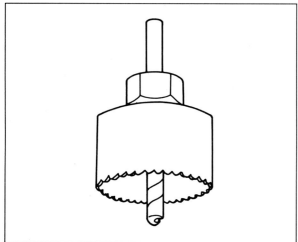

Figure C

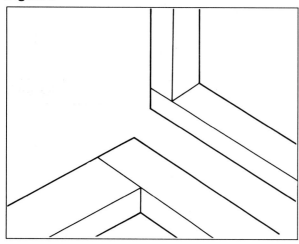

Figure D

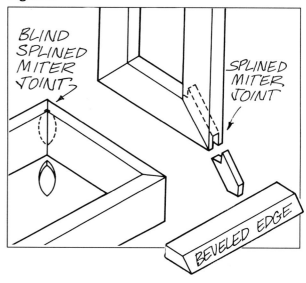

Fasteners and Other Hardware

While pure iron is quite resistant to rust, modern "iron" fasteners and hardware contain small amounts of carbon and are called "mild steel." Under outdoor (damp) conditions, mild steel eventually will rust away. More durable substances from which fasteners and hardware are made include brass, bronze, and alloyed stainless steel, although none is one-hundred percent rustproof. Your best bet will be galvanized mild-steel hardware, which is commonly available. If you can't find galvanized hardware, look for a rust-inhibiting product with which to coat steel hardware.

For a finished look, screws may be countersunk. Although this is a more common procedure for indoor furnishings and is not really necessary for more rustic outdoor projects, it will prevent the possibility of friends and family sustaining scratches caused by slightly protruding screw heads. In the same vein, finishing nails may be recessed but common nails usually are not. If you countersink the screws, the recesses may be filled with wooden plugs or wood filler. Wooden plugs will be almost invisible if you cut them from stock that matches the grain of the surrounding wood. This is easy to do, using a plug cutter (**Figure B**). Plugs also can be made by cutting slices from dowel rod, but they present end grain and will be much more apparent, particularly if the wood is stained.

Cutting and Joining

Butt Joints: A butt joint normally connects the end of one piece to the surface or edge of another (**Figure C**). The end grain of one piece will always show. Because there are no cuts made to form interlocking portions, this is an extemely weak joint. A butt joint can be strengthened using glue blocks, splines, nails, screws, dowels, or other reinforcement.

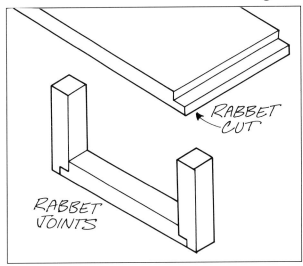

RABBET CUT

RABBET JOINTS

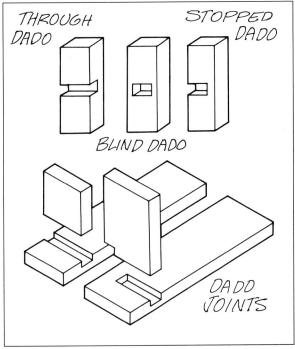

THROUGH DADO

STOPPED DADO

BLIND DADO

DADO JOINTS

Miters and Bevels: A miter joint connects two angle-cut ends (**Figure D**). It conceals the end grain of both pieces and can be reinforced using splines, dowels, or fasteners. The most common miter is a 45-degree, which is used to construct right-angle assemblies. A bevel is an angle cut made along an edge or surface.

Rabbets: A rabbet is an L-shaped groove and has many applications. A rabbet cut into one or both pieces to be joined conceals the end grain of one piece and allows for a greater surface area to be glued, thus creating a stronger joint (**Figure E**). This joint is commonly used for cabinet sides, and for box, case, and drawer construction. Normally it is reinforced using screws or nails. A rabbet cut has other uses such as recessing the inside of a door to fit into the door opening.

Dado: Basically, a dado is a groove. Several types of dadoes and dado joints are illustrated in **Figure F**. A through dado extends all the way from edge to edge (or end to end). A stopped dado extends from one edge to a point short of the opposite edge. A blind dado is stopped short of both edges.

Lap Joints: A lap joint normally is used to connect two members at right angles. In the most common lap joint, the two joined surfaces are flush (**Figure G**). This joint provides a large area to be glued.

Mortise and Tenon Joints: There are lots of variations on this theme, but the basic garden-variety mor-

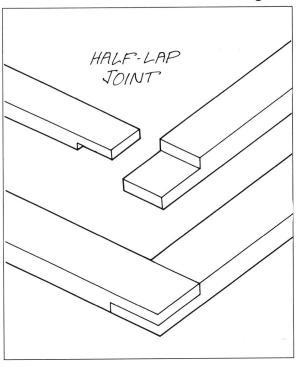

HALF-LAP JOINT

Figure H

THROUGH MORTISE AND TENON JOINT

BLIND MORTISE AND TENON JOINT

Figure I

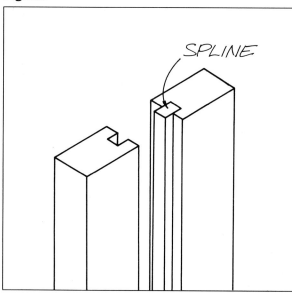

SPLINE

Figure J

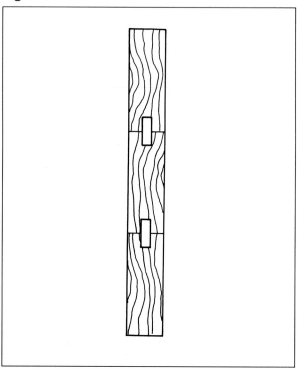

tise and tenon joints are shown in **Figure H**. This is an extremely strong joint and can be made even stronger. A pegged (or pinned) mortise and tenon joint is one in which the tenon extends out beyond the mortise and is itself mortised to accommodate a peg. The unglued, pegged mortise and tenon is a handy joint to use in furniture that you wish to disassemble for portability.

Spline Joints: A spline is a thin strip of wood used as a connecting member between two boards. It fits into dadoes cut into the edges to be joined, and can be used to strengthen any type of joint. A spline joint is shown in **Figure I**. Through splines reach from end to end. Blind splines are stopped short of the ends and cannot be seen once the joint is assembled.

Splines are specified in this book to create large parts (such as cabinet or box walls) that require several edge-joined boards to achieve the width. A splined edge joint is much stronger than one which is simply glued and clamped. Unglued splines create a structure that can expand and contract with atmospheric conditions without cracking or splitting. Unglued splines can be used, of course, only for parts that are secured at the ends to trim or other structures. In the boards that are splined together to form a wall, for instance, the splines usually may be left unglued since the wall is attached on all four edges to other structures. When edge-joining, every other board should be turned so that the ray patterns are alternated (**Figure J**) to avoid warping.

CONSTRUCTION TIPS

Working with Concrete

The main consideration in starting any outdoor project is the weather. Nothing will take the zip out of your hammer-banging faster than rain running down your neck. Concrete, for all its strength, is especially touchy about getting too wet, too dry, too hot or too cold.

If you find yourself with fresh concrete and sub-freezing or excessively hot temperatures, you can still save all your hard work by covering it with burlap, rags, and newspapers.

Concrete must also be allowed to "cure" properly for strength and durability. This means not allowing the concrete to dry too quickly. Cover the concrete with burlap and keep it soaked for five days when temperatures are 70 degrees F. or higher, and seven days when temperatures are below 70.

If you need only small amounts of cement you might consider dry ready-mixed concrete. This comes in bags ready for you to add water, and use. This stuff is not cheap however, so if your plans call for more than a single cubic yard of concrete you may wish to consider wet ready-mix. This is the "goop" that comes in those big trucks. When we say "big" we're talking thirty tons, so you don't want him cruising across your driveway and freshly sodded lawn. Because most outdoor building takes place in your back yard you may have to take it a wheelbarrow at a time from the truck to your building site so get help – if the driver has to wait you will be charged extra.

To calculate how much ready-mix cement you will need for a given project refer to the table on this page (**Figure K**).

A third alternative is to rent a small mixer and learn to mix your own. If you go for this option the formula is: 3 parts gravel or rock to 2 parts sand to 1 part dry cement – sounds like a delicious recipe doesn't it?

Be careful not to add too much water or you'll end up with gray soup that will take forever to dry, and when it does all the gravel and sand will be at the bottom. Just add a little water at a time, mixing as you go. It's a lot easier to add water than to take it out. Taking water out of cement is something like driving nails with your head: you can but you're not going to enjoy it.

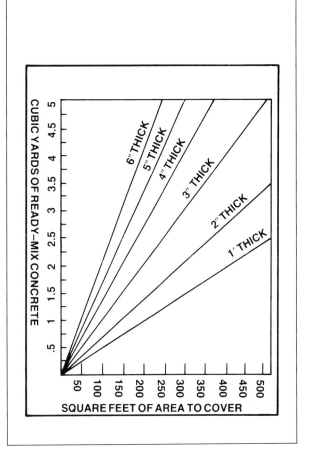

Setting Posts and Footings

The foundation of your outdoor structure is the least seen but most important part to be considered and planned. Whether it be for your fence or deck footing, if your foundation isn't secure, all the hard work you put into the structure could end up a part of your neighbor's yard decor with the first good breeze.

Whenever using wood in an outdoor structure, damaging insects and rotting caused by moisture can cause an early end for your project. Treated wood is available through many lumber yards or you can treat your own using pentachlorophenol ("penta") or creosote. The traditional means of avoiding this problem is by using redwood or cedar which are less prone to rotting but often harder to find or excessively expensive.

The important thing to consider when thinking price for materials is: is it cheaper to build it right the first time, or have to re-build every few years? If you translate your time and effort into dollars, the price of quality materials gets cheaper all the time.

The first step is to lay out the planned location of your structure. Make sure you check your property and easement lines and it's a good idea to have the utility companies come out and flag where any underground lines are. Tapping into the water lines can make your yard into a mini-Yellow Stone Park; hitting a sewer or septic line will make you very unpopular in the neighborhood; putting a shovel through "Ma Bell's" property can leave you rather isolated for a few days; and finding the electric or gas companies hidden goodies....we don't even want to think about that one! If you are planning on pouring a concrete slab, don't forget that if any of these utilities have to be dug up at a later date your structure may go under the shovel.

The utility companies are really very cooperative about letting you know where they have buried treasure so take advantage of it, besides, all the little multi-colored flags are kind of pretty.

Once you have the EXACT location of your structure plotted out, you have to decide where the posts (in the case of fencing) or footings (for decks or foundations) will need to be. If you are pouring a solid slab of concrete this will be where you will put up the forms.

Setting Fence Posts

Because a fence usually follows your property lines, you want to be especially careful that your fence doesn't lapse over into your neighbors yard. If you can find existing property markers great, if you can't you may find it cheaper to have a professional surveyor re-mark your boundaries than to have to move your fence later on. Once you have the property lines established it's then a good idea to plan your fence a good six-inches inside that line just to be safe.

Drive wooden stakes into the corners of your property (or at either end of where you plan to put the fence) and tie a taught string between the two points. At these corners, on either side of any gates, and at intervals of six to eight feet you will need at least 4x4-inch posts for

strength. Standard lumber comes in lengths of 6-, 8-, 12-, 14-, and 16-foot lengths so you should not have any waste in assembling the cross bars to go between your posts if you are careful in your post placement.

There are four methods for setting your fence posts: Setting the post in concrete; making a concrete collar around the post at the surface; by nailing a cleat or crossbar to the bottom of the post; or simply tamping the soil back into place around the post. Using any of these methods, you should plan on setting the posts into the ground at least ⅓ of their total length — for example, if you want a six-foot high fence you should plan on buying nine-foot posts, burying them three feet into the ground.

Setting the posts in concrete is by far the preferred method. Using concrete, you should dig the hole in a bell shape, bigger at the bottom than at the top, and be sure it is deeper than the frost-line in your area. The reason for this shape and depth is that freezing water which may have seeped under and around the concrete will "heave" or push the concrete, post, and the whole bloomin' fence right up out of the ground.

Making a concrete collar involves tamping soil around the post up to a few inches of the surface. Then a ring of concrete is poured around the post extending above the surface where it is shaped into a cone to allow for the runoff of water.

When using concrete with your fenceposts it is recommended that you allow five days to a week for the concrete to dry completely before attaching the rails and fencing.

If you have a well drained and firm soil or are putting up a light weight fence such as latticework, you may wish to simply place the posts over a few inches of gravel and tamp the soil back into place around them. If water tends to stand in your yard, however, your posts will be more subject to rotting.

Nailing cleats to the bottom of the post anchors the post more securely than tamping alone but has the same disadvantage in allowing rotting of the post when subject to ground water. Using this method also requires you to dig a much bigger hole to bury the cleat. If your fence is to be very long you'll quickly discover that digging post holes is not exactly one of lifes more enjoyable pastimes.

Footings and Posts for Decking

When you consider that you are going to be walking around on a surface that is supported by these posts, the importance of solid foundation becomes a main concern. As a matter of fact, it is so important that the methods used for fence posts aren't even considered for decking.

There are basically only three methods that you should consider: posts set into concrete filled fiber forms which themselves extend above ground level; setting the post into concrete filled holes with a good portion of concrete extending above ground level; or building forms around the surface opening of a hole, filling to the top of the form with concrete and mounting the post atop this pedestal. Again, dig the holes to a level below frost line to prevent heaving.

Waxed fiber forms can be purchased in several diameters and cut to any length you need. Simply dig a hole, drop the cylinder in making sure several inches extend above the ground, pour in five or six inches of concrete and allow this to dry. Then set your post into the cylinder and fill around the post and the cylinder with more concrete, tappering the top so that water will run off.

If your soil is sandy or otherwise will not stay tight enough to keep from falling into the hole you have dug, the method using the fiber form is best.

The method of setting posts into concrete filled holes in the ground is the least preferred of the three methods listed here. Some seepage of water is sure to occur with time (waxed forms slow this process to some degree) and rotting will follow.

Again pour several inches of concrete into the bottom of the hole and allow this to dry. Then position the post and fill to the top of the forms with more concrete, tappering the top for runoff. The raised portion will protect the post from moisture and insects.

The more preferred method is to use either of the two previous methods to form a pedestal. The post is not set INTO the concrete but rather on top of it.

There are several methods of securing the post to the concrete pedestal. The footings shown in **Figure L** are examples of some of these methods. These methods have several advantages over either of the methods involving setting the posts below ground level. For one

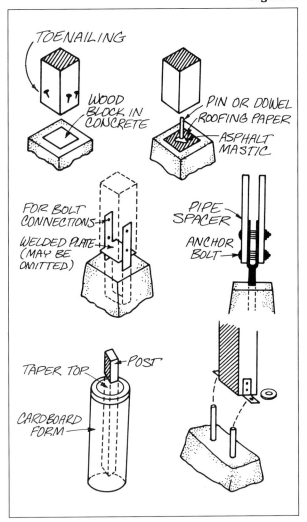

Figure L

is that it is easier to work with the posts, leveling and measuring, when it is not literally "set in stone." Perhaps the biggest advantage is that, if bad came to worse, you could disconnect and move your structure by simply taking it off of the footings.

Whichever method you choose, make sure your posts are aligned with one another and perpendicular. If you're setting the posts in the concrete, brace the posts securely until the concrete dries. Failure to accomplish this will result in the post having uneven and undue stress causing the post to bow and possibly break or twist off of its footing.

Bricklaying For Outdoor Barbecues

Before you take the Buick down to your local building supply dealer to pick up a load of brick for your barbeque, there are a few things you should know about.

For one thing, the family station wagon is going to complain terribly about lugging bricks and mortar around town. See if the dealer will deliver. If they will, you can deduct the price of a new set of shock absorbers from the total cost of your barbecue.

Bricks

If you have ever shopped for lumber (or read the section of Tips and Techniques on lumber grades) you know that wood comes in various qualities as well as quantities. Buying brick has the same considerations.

Standard brick is considered 8 to 8¼ inches in length, 3¾ to 3⅞ inches in width, and 2¼ to 2½ inches in depth. These dimensions may vary as much as ½ inch even between batches at the same supplier, so check out the actual size of the brick before calculating how much you are going to buy. If your brick is within "standard" sizes, you can estimate the number of bricks you will need. Figure (from your own plans) the number of square feet of surface in the walls of your barbecue (or anything else you're building) and multiply by 6½ if your walls are to be one brick in width. Double that factor (13) if the walls are to be two bricks in width, and so on. (**Note:** This formula is valid considering a ½-inch inch layer of mortar between bricks.)

You will find that bricks also come in varying degrees of hardness. A "well-burned" brick will withstand heat better than a "green" brick. You can generally tell how hard-burned a brick is by striking it with a hammer. A green brick will give off a dull thud, while a well-burned brick will ring when struck.

If you plan on using an inside layer of fire-brick, the hardness of the outside layer really doesn't matter as much. If fire-brick is not to be used, you will definately want the hardest brick you can get. Green brick will crack or even explode if subjected to too much heat.

Mortar for Bricklaying

Mortar is a mixture of cement, fine sand, a small amount of lime or fireclay, and water. Fireclay will serve just as well as lime, so in structures subject to heat it is definatly recommended since it is heat resistant.

The recommended formula for fireclay-cement mortar is: 1 part cement; 4½ parts clean, fine sand; and ½ part fireclay (substitute ½ part lime for lime-cement mortar). If you don't want to mix your own ingredients you can buy dry-mix mortar that is a fireclay mixture. This dry-mix is quite a bit more expensive than buying the ingredients seperately, but it does make the job a lot easier.

A sack of ready-mix mortar will suffice for about 50 bricks. If you are going to mix your own ingredients, use approximately one 100 pound sack of cement, 4 ½ cu.ft. of sand, and one 50 pound sack of fireclay or lime, for every 250 bricks.

Whichever way you choose, ready-mix or mix-your-own, mix only a small portion of the ingredients with water at a time so the mortar doesn't dry up before you have a chance to use it. If you are mixing your own ingedients, use a shovelful of cement, 4 ½ shovelfuls of sand and ½ shovelful of fireclay or lime at a time. Mix the ingredients together while still dry, then scoop out a small hollow in the center and add a little water. Continue blending and adding water until the mortar slips cleanly off of the mixing tool (the same is true for ready-mix). If the mixture begins to dry out while you're still using it, add a little more water. You want to be able to use the whole batch within an hour.

Tools

To lay bricks you will need a couple of special tools and several ordinary ones.

Tools you may not have around the house, unless you have layed brick before, include: a sturdy, pointed trowel with a ten-inch blade, and a broad-bladed cold chisel known as a "brick set" for cutting bricks (refer to **Figure M**).

The household variety of tools include: a hammer; a level; a carpenter's square; a length of string; and a piece of straight wooden board at least 3-feet long to set the level on.

The Foundation

The first step in building your barbecue, after you have planned out the size and shape, is to make a foundation for the bricks to sit on. The best, and one of the easiest methods is to set up forms and pour a concrete slab. Make sure this slab has a level surface and is at least 4 to 6-inches thick to prevent cracking. Once this has thoroughly dried you're ready to mix your mortar (don't take the steaks out of the freezer just yet).

Laying the Bricks

Common bricks (NOT firebrick) should be slightly damp when they are laid. Spray the bricks with water at least four hours before you plan on starting. If they are too wet they will dilute the mortar and tend to slide before the mortar can set properly.

When you're ready to start, spread a trowel-full of mortar, ½-inch thick on the slab where you plan to set the brick. Until you get the hang of it, spread only one bricks worth of mortar at a time. Now press the brick firmly in place and trim off the excess mortar and spread it on the end of the brick that will join the next brick. Set one entire layer, using the carpenter's square to make sure the corners are at right angles.

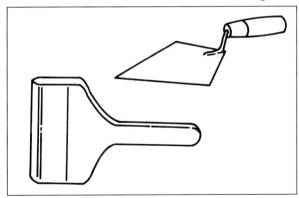

It is best to next set up the corners by laying up two or three rows at right angles to each other (see **Figure N**). Continually check with the level and square to make sure you are getting everything right. Set up one corner at a time and then move on to the next. run a guideline between each corner and fill-in between the corners. Be sure the bricks overlap a full brick for every vertical joint.

Figure N

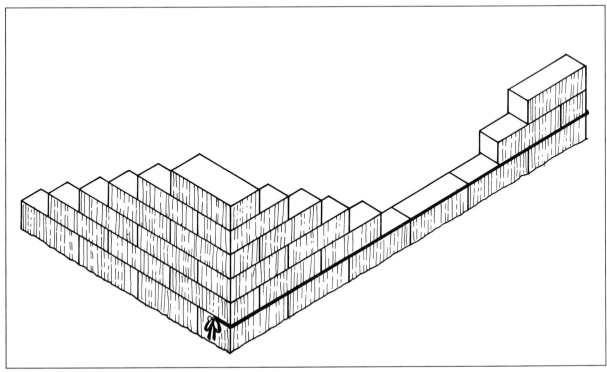

Figure O

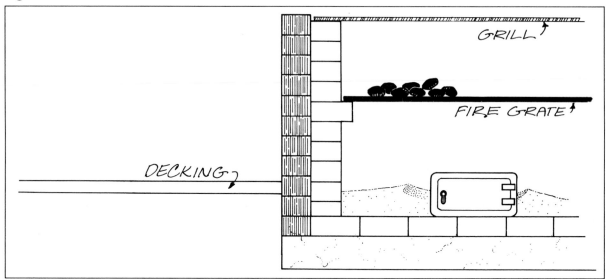

Remember to check your level every so often by placing the board over a finished row and setting the level on top.

Continue to build up the corners, then filling in-between, until your barbecue is at the desired height.

If you have to cut any bricks to fit, use the brick set and hammer. Hold the brick set against the brick with the beveled side towards the end you are going to cut off. Tapping the set lightly, cut a groove along each side, then place the set in the original position and hit it sharply with the hammer.

Firebrick

Firebricks are made from a type of clay that can withstand high temperatures that would normally destroy common brick and are used to line the interior of barbecues and fireplaces.

There are a few variations in the technique for laying firebrick which differ from those used for common brick: never dampen firebrick before setting them, they should be completely dry; use a very thin layer of mortar ($1/16$ to $1/4$-inch) and always use fireclay-cement mortar; lay the bricks on their edges rather on their sides — you will have to use fewer bricks and they will still provide plenty of insulation; firebricks are larger and heavier than common bricks. The standard size for firebrick is 9 x 4½ x 2½-inches, so make your calculations accordingly, before you buy.

Although firebrick is very heat resistant, it does not stand up well when exposed to extreme cold or moisture. Ask your local dealer about firebrick durability in your area. If you are in the northern portion of the country, a double layer of hard-burned brick may be more suitable for a barbecue exposed to the elements.

When installing the firebrick lining for your barbecue, don't forget to provide some sort of support for the fire grate and the grill. This can be accomplished by simply setting a layer of brick on its side extending into the fire pit upon which the metal grate and grill can rest (see **Figure O**).

The Hard Part

Once you have your barbecue finished you should allow the assembly to dry for at least two weeks. After that, build several small fires in the barbecue to properly "cure" the mortar. THEN break out the steaks (don't forget to send me an invitation).

If your barbecue is to be exposed to the elements, cover it with plastic if possible. Water has a nasty habit of expanding when frozen or turned to steam. When that water has crept between the bricks in your barbecue you may find yourself re-building after every heavy rain storm.

Building Site Drainage

Because most outdoor structures are made of wood, their biggest enemy is rot caused by moisture and insects. After the next hard rain go out to your planned building site and probe around in the dirt. If one side of your yard seems dryer than another, the water probably is settling at a natural low point. If that low point happens to be where you want your deck or building, then you are going to have to do a little extra work before you start the project.

The French drain (**Figure P**) is a simple process used by landscape architects and builders to keep water from collecting in any spot or area without having to change the entire grade of the property. All you need is a shovel, gravel, and lengths of PVC pipe with holes drilled along one side.

Start by digging a trench at least twelve to eighteen inches deep, running away from the area you wish to drain. Since you want to drain the water away from instead of towards your low spot, the ditch will need to run slightly downhill, which means digging deeper as you go. Depending on how much of a drainage problem you have, you may need to run more than one line radiating away from the problem area.

The next step in the French drain is to pour several inches (4 to 6) of gravel into the bottom of the ditch. Over the bed of gravel lay in the lengths of PVC pipe, turned so the side drilled with holes is facing up. Pour in more gravel until the pipe is buried and fill the ditch the rest of the way to the surface with the original soil.

If the drainage problem isn't very severe, the same effect can be achieved without using PVC pipe or digging an extremely deep ditch. Dig the ditch about 1 foot deep and several inches across and refill to the top with gravel. Your grass will cover the gravel in one summer and you'll never be able to tell where it is.

If it simply isn't possible or practical to run long drainage lines through your yard, a good alternative is to dig several deep wells (4 feet or deeper, depending on the amount of drainage needed) and refill the holes with loose rock, gravel, or broken bits of brick. These two methods can be combined, using wells and short sections of drainage pipe to cover a larger area.

I know very few people whose favorite hobby is digging ditches, so you may wish to hire the job out to

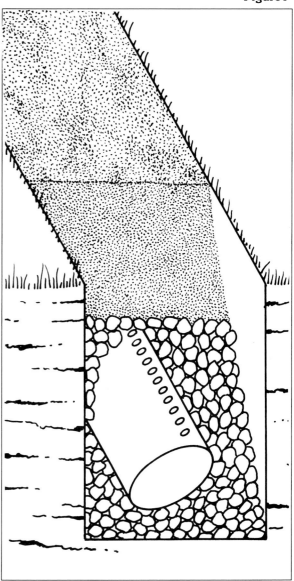

Figure P

someone who has a ditching machine or backhoe. They will be able to knock out the job in a fraction of the time that it will take you to do it by hand. Don't forget to have the utility companies mark the locations of their buried "goodies." You will want to have this done in the area of your building site anyway, so you don't have any unpleasant surprises when digging footings or pouring slabs.

Roofing

Roofing is so amazingly simple that it can almost be explained in one word – overlap. No matter whether you choose asphalt, wood, asbestos, tile, aluminum, or slate shingles, the process is very similar. You start at the bottom and work your way up!

1. Roll out roofing felt over the plywood sheeting, going ACROSS the roof, not up and down. Just as with the shingles, start at the bottom and overlap each layer as you go up the roof.

2. Attach the first row of shingles slightly overlapping the eave of the roof. Go completely across the roof before starting the next row. This first row of shingles should be doubled – that is attach another layer of shingles directly over the first to make a double layer at the eave.

3. As each row overlaps the previous row, make sure that the slots (in asphalt shingles) and the points where the shingles butt together (side by side) do not match the same points on the row underneath (**Figure Q**). This will mean cutting the first, and possibly the last, shingle in a row. The amount of overlap for each row of shingles will vary according to the type and manufacture of the shingles. Asphalt shingles commonly overlap the previous row by seven inches, leaving five inches exposed in each row.

Figure R

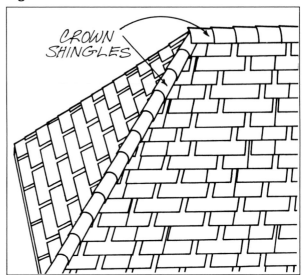

4. When the peak, or crown of the roof is reached, use crown shingles. ALL sides of the roof are covered before the crown shingles are applied. If the crown shingles are run vertically, such as in our Gazebo plans, the crown shingles overlap starting at the bottom of the roof. At the peak of the roof the crown shingles are overlapped horizontally, unlike the normal shingles that butt side by side (**Figure R**).

Figure Q

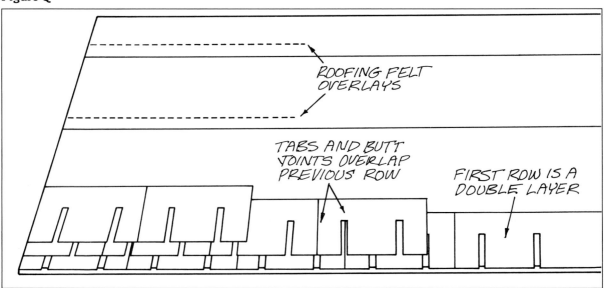

Projects

Latticework Barbecue Center

Have you ever charcoaled dinner in the garage because it was raining outside? Somehow, charcoaling hamburgers and smoking the windows of your car at the same time seems to take the fun out of dinner. Our solution: the latticework barbecue center. We started out just trying to keep our charcoal dry, but ended up with a great-looking piece of yard decor at a very attractive cost. The entire 4 x 7-foot structure is made from redwood and takes only a weekend or two to complete. If you feel like you need a little more elbow room, these plans can be expanded to any size you wish.

Figure A

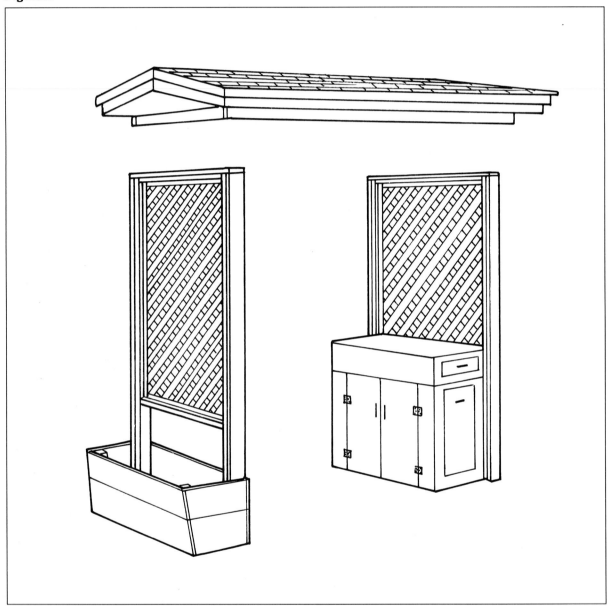

The barbecue center is built in three major sections (**Figure A**): the planter/lattice wall; the storage cabinet/lattice wall; and the roof. These sections are built separately and then assembled to create the finished barbecue center. A materials list and a parts list are given for each individual section.

THE PLANTER/LATTICE WALL

The planter/lattice wall is a very simple three-sided frame built from 2 x 4s and 1 x 2s, enclosing a latticework panel constructed from ⅛ x 1½-inch strips ripped from 2 x 6 redwood boards. The planter is made from 1 x 8 redwood and is attached around and to the lattice wall posts. To better illustrate the planter assembly we have labeled the various planter pieces.

Materials

8 linear feet of 2 x 6 redwood
44 linear feet of 2 x 4 redwood
3 linear feet of 2 x 2 redwood
22 linear feet of 1 x 8 redwood
33 linear feet of 1 x 2 redwood
3d finishing nails
4d and 8d common nails
Small brads or staples

Cutting the Wood

1. Cut the parts listed below from the specified materials. Label the parts.

Part	Length	Quantity	Material
For the wall frame:			
Posts	76 inches	2	2 x 4
Posts	74½ inches	2	2 x 4
Top Support	48 inches	1	2 x 4
Rails	42 inches	2	2 x 4
Bottom Support	45 inches	1	2 x 4
Keepers	44½ inches	4	1 x 2
Keepers	42 inches	4	1 x 2
For the planter:			
A	14 inches	2	2 x 2
B	49½ inches	4	1 x 8
C	16¼ inches	2	1 x 8
D	15 inches	2	1 x 8

2. Modify both of the C pieces and both of the D pieces as shown in the scale drawing, **Figure K**.

3. Rip the 8-foot redwood 2 x 6 into ⅛ x 1½-inch lattice strips, 8 feet long. This should provide enough lattice for both the planter and cabinet walls.

Assembly

The Frame and Latticework

Refer to **Figure B** as you assemble the latticework wall.

Figure C

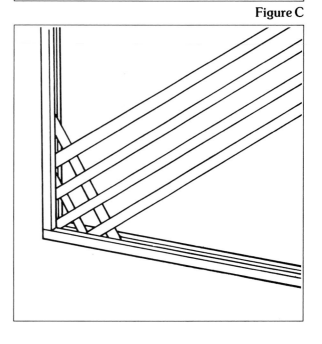

Figure D

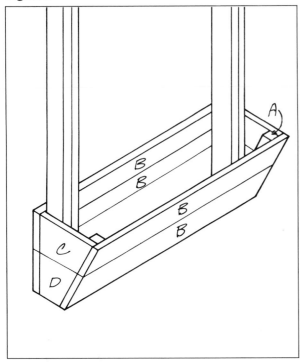

1. Starting with the Posts, nail a long Post to a short Post, wide sides together with one end flush. Repeat this step to make a second post.

2. Secure the two assembled posts together by nailing the Top Support across the flush ends, the two shorter legs of the posts being on the inside. At the opposite end attach the Bottom Support flush over the ends of the shorter post legs and butting against the longer post legs.

3. The Rails are attached to this assembly next. The first Rail is attached to the bottom of the Top Support piece, between the posts. The second Rail is nailed between the posts, 48 inches below the first. You should now have a 48 x 42-inch window in which the latticework panel will sit.

4. On a flat surface, construct one keeper frame, using two long and two short Keeper pieces (see **Figure C**). The outside dimensions of this frame should be the same as the inside dimensions of the window.

The diagonal measurement from one corner of the window to the other should be 64 inches. Cut a lattice

strip to this length and attach it from one corner of the keeper frame to the opposite corner using small brads or staples.

The next piece of lattice should be 6 inches shorter than the first. The third will be 7 inches shorter, the fourth 8 inches shorter, and so on. Attach these lattice strips to the keeper frame using a spare lattice strip as a spacer, until you reach the corners. Then reverse the diagonal and repeat the process to attach a second layer of strips. If the ends of the lattice extend beyond the outer edges of the keeper frame simply trim to fit after the panel is complete.

With the lattice in place, attach a second keeper frame, sandwiching the latticework between the two frames to form a latticework panel.

5. The latticework panel is now placed in the window $7/8$ inch from either edge and attached to the Posts and Rails by driving nails through the Keepers.

6. Measure 15 inches across the top of the wall from each end, and at each point drill a pilot hole $1\frac{1}{2}$ inches deep down into the Top Support piece. These holes will be used to attach the roof to the walls during the final assembly process.

The Planter

Refer to **Figure D** as you assemble the planter around the posts. We did not include a bottom in our planter because it rests directly on the ground. If your barbecue center is to sit on a patio, deck, or concrete slab you may wish to add a bottom or plastic liner. Just make sure there will be proper drainage.

1. Edge-glue two of the angled side pieces, placing the longer C piece over the shorter D, with edges flush. Along the inside of the angled edge attach the Planter Support A. Repeat this step to make a mirror image second side.

2. Glue two of the B pieces across the angled edges of the assembled side pieces so that the side pieces butt against the two front pieces B. Secure the corners by nailing through both of the front pieces B into the Planter Support A.

3. The assembled front-and-sides section is now attached to the outside of the posts, the rear edges of the sides being flush with the rear of the posts.

4. The remaining two B pieces form the back of the planter and are attached to the backs of the posts, flush with the planter sides which butt against it.

THE CABINET/LATTICE WALL

This wall is built in the same manner as the Planter/Lattice wall except that all four post legs are the same length and the latticework panel is shorter to allow for the cabinet. The cabinet provides a working surface, a drawer for long utensils, a charcoal bin, and a storage area underneath. To better illustrate the cabinet assembly we have labeled the various cabinet pieces.

Materials

36 linear feet of 1 x 2 redwood
4 linear feet of 1 x 3 redwood
13 linear feet of 1 x 4 redwood
13 linear feet of 1 x 5 redwood
3 linear feet of 1 x 6 redwood
60 linear feet of 1 x 8 redwood
2 linear feet of 2 x 2 redwood
54 linear feet of 2 x 4 redwood
16-inch length of ¾-inch wooden dowel
2 x 4-foot piece of ½-inch plywood
1 x 3-foot piece of ¼-inch plywood
6 linear feet of ½-inch square trim
15 linear feet of ½ x ¾-inch trim
Four 2 x 2-inch decorative hinges
Four ¾-inch conduit hangers
Four ⅜-inch-diameter lag bolts each 4 inches long
3d finishing nails
4d and 8d common nails
Small brads or staples
Carpenter's glue

Cutting the Wood

1. Cut the following pieces for the wall:

Part	Length	Quantity	Material
Posts	76 inches	4	2 x 4
Top Support	48 inches	1	2 x 4
Rail	42 inches	1	2 x 4
Keepers	42 inches	4	1 x 2
Keepers	37½ inches	4	1 x 2

2. Cut the following pieces for the cabinet, using the specified materials. Label the parts for reference later.

Part	Dimensions in inches	Quantity	Material
A Top	7¼ x 41¾	2	1 x 8
B Top	3 x 41¾	1	1 x 4
C Front	7¼ x 41¾	1	1 x 8
D Front	7¼ x 26	4	1 x 8
E Front	6¼ x 26	2	1 x 8
F Front	3½ x 12	4	1 x 4
G Back	7¼ x 33¼	5	1 x 8
H Back	5½ x 33¼	1	1 x 6
I Side	7¼ x 15¾	1	1 x 8
J Side	7¼ x 22¼	1	1 x 8
K Side	4⅜ x 22¼	1	1 x 5
L Side	2 x 22¼	2	1 x 3
M Side	3¼ x 11⅝	1	1 x 4
N Side	7¼ x 15¾	1	1 x 8
O Side	7¼ x 26	2	1 x 8
P Side	1¼ x 26	1	1 x 2
Q Side	3½ x 13	1	1 x 4
R Base	3½ x 37¼	2	2 x 4
S Base	3½ x 15¾	2	2 x 4
T Base	7¼ x 15¾	5	1 x 8
U Base	4 x 15¾	1	1 x 5
V Drawer	4 x 10⅜	2	1 x 5
W Drawer	4 x 30	2	1 x 5
X Drawer	10⅞ x 29	1	¼-inch ply
Y Drawer	½ x 30	2	½ x ½
Z Drawer	1⅜ x 40¼	2	2 x 4
AA Drawer	1½ x 40¼	1	1 x 2
BB Drawer	1½ x 13	1	2 x 2
CC Drawer	½ x 40¼	4	½ x ¾
DD Drawer	3½ x 13	1	1 x 4
EE Bin	7¼ x 22¼	1	1 x 8
FF Bin	4⅜ x 22¼	1	1 x 5
GG Bin	9 x 18	2	½-inch ply
HH Bin	6½ x 18	2	½-inch ply
II Bin	3 x 9	1	½-inch ply
JJ Bin	3½ x 7½	1	1 x 4

3. The **Q** and **HH** pieces must be altered slightly. Modify the **Q** piece and both **HH** pieces as indicated in the cutting diagrams, **Figure K**.

Figure E

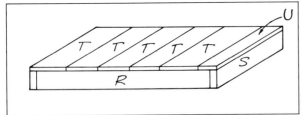

Figure F

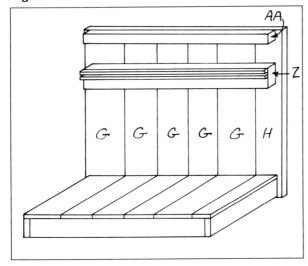

Figure G

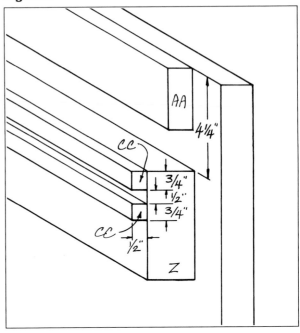

Assembly

The Cabinet

The cabinet is in itself a complete project. We found this part of our barbecue center so handy that we have used the same plans for an identical cabinet for the workshop. The charcoal bin makes a great mini-file cabinet for saving old plans, and the drawer is long enough to hide a good saw from those family members who think the ideal location for expensive tools is in the yard (where they are easily found with the lawn mower the following spring).

1. This part of the project starts from the ground up, with the base (refer to **Figure E**). Butt the two R pieces flush with the ends of the two S pieces to form a 15¾ x 40¼-inch rectangle. Over the top of this nail the five T pieces and the U piece. When finished all edges should be flush with the outside of the 2 x 4 base.

2. For the cabinet back, lay the five G pieces and the H piece side-by-side with the ends flush. Attach the AA piece (**Figure F**) across the width of the assembled pieces, ¾ inch from either side and flush with the tops.

3. One side of the drawer guide is now assembled on the back panel assembly (**Figure G**). Mount a Z piece to the back panel assembly, ¾ inch from either end and 4¼ inches from the top. Along the length of the Z piece and flush with its top, attach a CC Trim piece, placing the ¾-inch side against the Z piece, and another identical CC piece parallel to and ½ inch below the first.

4. The finished back can now be positioned along one long side of the base, allowing the back panel to overlap the base ¾ inch at either end. Nail the panel in place.

5. The front of the cabinet (**Figure H**) is assembled using a C piece for the upper portion, under which are attached two vertical D pieces, flush with the ends of the C piece. These pieces are secured to one another using a Z piece mounted along the length of the horizontal C piece, 4¼ inches from the top and centered ¾ inch from either end. This will overlap the vertical pieces by ½ inch.

Figure H

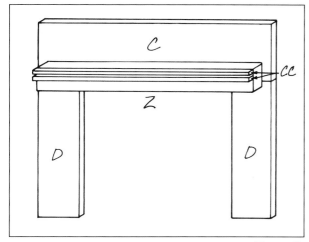

Figure I

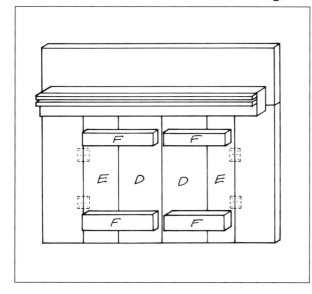

Figure J

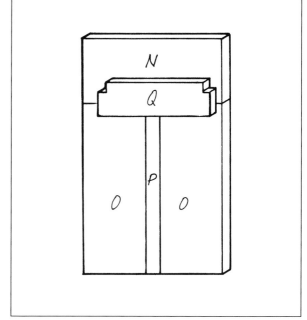

6. To the face of the Z piece attach two CC Trim pieces for drawer guides, in the same manner as in step 3 (**Figure G**).

7. The cabinet doors (**Figure I**) are each made from one D piece and one E piece. Secure the pieces together using two F pieces. The doors are mounted to the front panel using decorative hinges.

8. The cabinet front assembly can now be mounted to the base, allowing a ¾ inch overlap at either end of the base.

9. The left side of the cabinet (**Figure J**) is made using the two O pieces, one on either side of a P piece, all three butted against the bottom edge of a horizontal N piece. These pieces are joined from the back using a Q piece (see cutting diagram, **Figure K**).

10. Arrange the four side pieces face down on a flat surface. Position the connecting Q piece 4½ inches from the top of the upper N piece and 1½ inches in from either outer edge of the O pieces. Glue and nail the connecting Q piece to all four facing pieces.

11. The left side assembly can now be mounted to the base between the front and back panels. Secure all three panels (front, back, and side) by driving finishing nails through the front and back panels and into the side panel. When in place, the side panel Q piece should act as additional support for the drawer guides attached to the front and back panels.

12. The right side of the cabinet (having the drawer and charcoal bin) is mounted to the cabinet assembly in individual pieces instead of as a complete panel. The first phase of this is to mount the BB piece between the Z pieces attached to the front and back panels. This 2 x 2 BB piece should butt against the Z pieces flush with

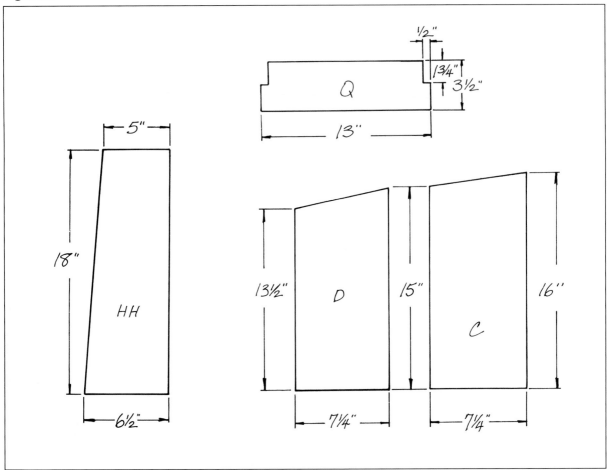

Figure L

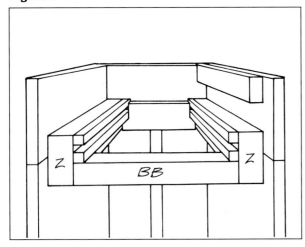

the ends and directly below the **CC** drawer guides (see **Figure L**).

13. The drawer facing is cut directly from the center of the **I** piece. Measure in 1⅜ inches from all four sides and mark out a 4½ x 13-inch rectangular drawer face. If you can make this cut without damaging either the facing or the surrounding frame you have our total admiration. We ended up cutting the frame from one piece and the drawer facing from another. Whichever the case, the outer drawer frame is now positioned between the front and back panels, flush with the tops of both. Glue and nail the frame to the **BB** piece and the **Z** pieces mounted on the front and back panels and then nail through the front and back panels.

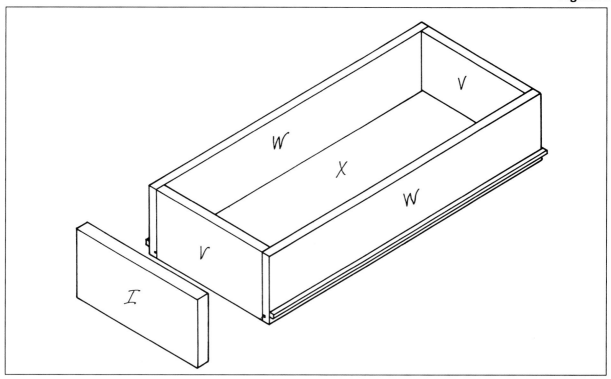

14. The drawer itself (**Figure M**) is made from two W sides and two V ends. All of the drawer side and end pieces are grooved their entire length, ¼ inch from the bottom edge, the groove itself being ¾ inch wide and deep. The drawer is now assembled around the X plywood piece that rests in the grooves providing the drawer bottom. The Trim pieces (**Y**) are now mounted down the length of the drawer sides, ⅜ inch from the lower edge to serve as the drawer runner. The last step is to attach the drawer face, cut from the I piece, to one end of the drawer assembly. Glue the drawer assembly ⅜ inch down from the facing top and ½ inch from either side. Now slide that devil in and see how it fits! If it seems a little too snug, simply sand a bit off of the drawer runners.

15. Two L pieces are now mounted below the drawer frame to form the frame sides for the charcoal bin (**Figure N**). These pieces are nailed at the bottom to the base, at the top to the Z pieces, and to the front and back panels.

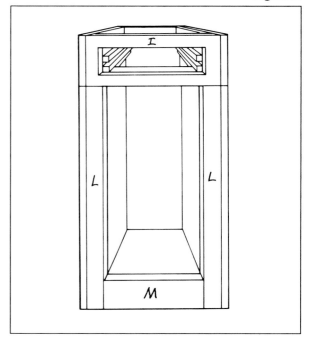

Figure O

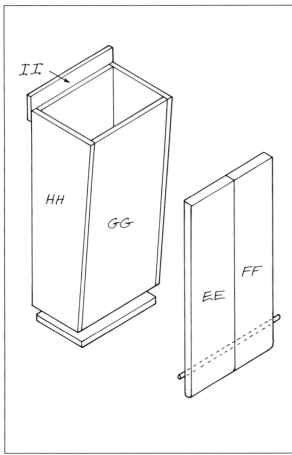

Figure P

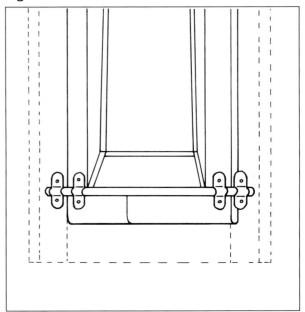

Figure Q

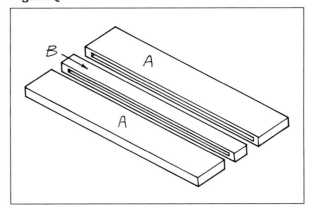

16. The **M** piece is next attached between the bin frame sides at the bottom of the bin opening. Nail this piece directly to the base.

17. The charcoal bin is a wedge-shaped box (**Figure O**) with plywood ends **HH** and sides **GG**, a 1 x 4 bottom **JJ** piece, and an open top. The plywood **II** piece is mounted at the top of the back **GG** piece extending 2 inches above the bin to act as a stop (so the bin doesn't fall out on your toes).

18. The bin face is made from one **EE** piece and one **FF** piece set side by side and attached directly to the bin assembly. The bin assembly is mounted 2½ inches down from the top of the bin face and 1 inch from either side. The bottom edge of the bin face is rounded so as not to bind when the bin is opened.

19. The assembled bin is hinged to the cabinet by a 16-inch length of ¾-inch wooden dowel and four ¾-inch conduit hangers attached to the back of the bin face below the bin itself and the ends of the dowel inside the cabinet **L** pieces (**Figure P**).

20. The cabinet top (**Figure Q**) is constructed of two **A** pieces, one on either side of a **B** piece. The pieces are joined by blind splines. The top should overhang the front of the cabinet by ¼ inch with all other edges flush with the sides and back. Drive finishing nails through the top into the panels it rests on.

Figure R

The Wall

To build the Cabinet/Lattice Wall refer back to the Planter/Lattice Wall assembly steps (**Figure B**). There are the following variations between the two walls that must be taken into account:

1. The Posts are all 76 inches in length and will be joined flush at either end.

2. There is only one Rail instead of two. The lower Rail (beneath the lattice panel) is replaced by the cabinet (**Figure R**).

3. The lattice panel (including keeper frame) is $40\frac{3}{4}$ inches long from top to bottom instead of 48 inches long (see **Figure A**). To make sure the cabinet will fit under the lattice panel, measure the exact height of your cabinet. This must be the distance from the bottom of the posts to the lattice panel.

4. There is no planter at this end, the cabinet occupies this space.

Joining the Cabinet and Wall

The finished cabinet should now fit under the lattice panel wall with the lattice panel coming to rest along the back edge of the cabinet and the posts fitting flush along either side. When positioning the cabinet between the posts make sure you do not insert the cabinet so far that the drawer is blocked from opening. Drill through the posts and into the sides of the cabinet, inserting 4-inch lag bolts to secure the two pieces together.

THE ROOF

The roof joists will sit directly on top of the planter and cabinet lattice walls.

Materials

45 linear feet of 2 x 4 redwood
26 linear feet of 1 x 4 redwood
22 linear feet of $\frac{1}{2}$ x 1-inch redwood trim
40 square feet of $\frac{1}{4}$-inch exterior grade plywood
Two bundles of shingles
Roofing felt
Four $\frac{3}{8}$-inch-diameter lag bolts each 5 inches long
4d and 8d common nails

Cutting the Wood

Cut the following pieces:

Part	Material	Length	Quantity
Rafters	2 x 4	$27\frac{3}{4}$ inches	6
Peak	2 x 4	7 feet	1
Plates	2 x 4	7 feet	2
Joists	2 x 4	45 inches	2
Extensions	2 x 4	$5\frac{1}{2}$-inches	4
Gables	1 x 4	$28\frac{1}{2}$ inches	4
Eaves	1 x 4	8 feet	2
Trim	$\frac{1}{2}$ x 1	$29\frac{1}{2}$ inches	2
Trim	$\frac{1}{2}$ x 1	$97\frac{1}{2}$ inches	2
Roof	ply	96 x 30 inches	2

Figure S

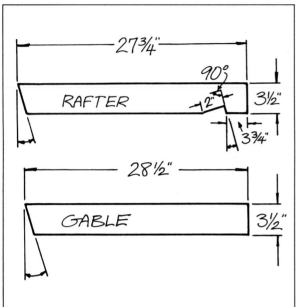

27¾"

90°

RAFTER

2"

3½"

3¾"

28½"

GABLE

3½"

Assembly

1. The roof structure begins by attaching the two Joists between and at either end of the Plates to form a 4 x 7-foot rectangle. Measure in 15 inches from both ends of the Joists (4-foot side) and drill a pilot hole down into the top and completely through the Joist. Repeat this to make four holes (two to a side) which will be used when attaching the finished roof to the walls.

2. The Rafter ends are cut at a 10-degree angle to meet with the Peak. The Rafter seat (the point where the Rafter rests on the Plate) is also cut at a 10-degree angle (see **Figure S**).

3. Toenail the Rafters to the 7-foot-long Peak, one pair at either end and one pair in the middle (see **Figure T**). Secure the Rafter seats along the Plate.

4. Attached to the Rafters and extending outward from either end mount the two Extensions to which the 1 x 4 Gables will attach (see **Figure T**).

Figure T

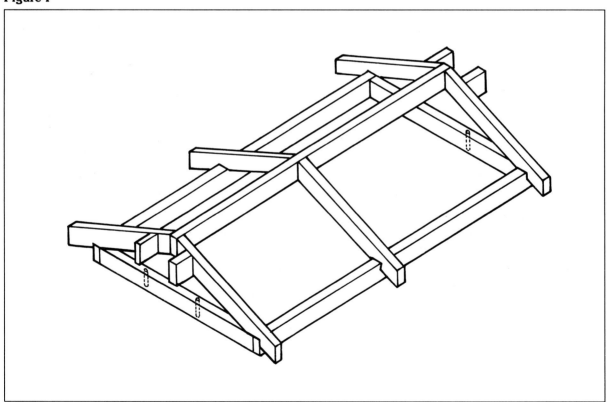

5. Attach the Gable pieces to the Extensions. The peaked ends of the Gables are cut at a 10-degree angle to match the cut of the roof (see **Figure U**). They should run parallel to the Rafters.

6. Attach the Eave pieces to the foot of the Rafters so that the ends of the Eaves are flush with the Gable pieces.

7. The Trim pieces are next attached to the Gable and Eave pieces, flush with the tops.

8. You are now ready to attach the plywood sheeting to the roof. Each 8-foot x 30-inch piece will cover one side of the roof. Where the panels meet at the peak there may be a small gap but don't worry about it – the roofing felt and shingles will cover it.

9. See the Tips & Techniques section on roofing.

Final Assembly

The last stage (after you get the hamburger out of the freezer) is to put the planter/lattice wall, the cabinet/lattice wall, and the roof sections together. You may need to take out a little extra hamburger because you will need a couple of assistants.

1. Position the two end walls at the location you want the barbecue center, 7 feet apart (measure the outside edge post to post).

2. With help (unless you are VERY strong), lift the roof section over the walls allowing the Joists to come to rest on the tops of the walls.

3. Use a level to get the walls straight and align the holes drilled in the Joists and the wall tops (**Figure V**).

Figure U

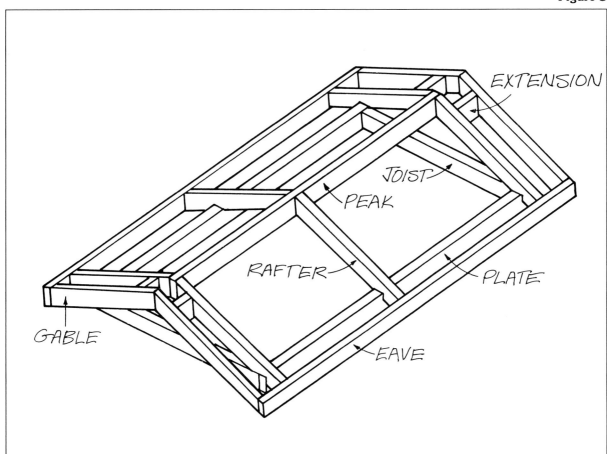

Figure V

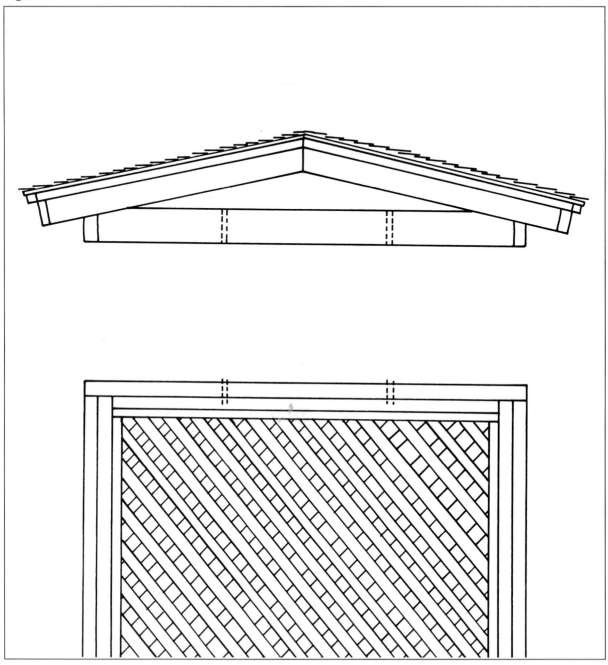

4. Insert the five-inch-long lag bolts through the roof Joists and into the Tops of the walls. Note: If you live in an area subject to heavy snows or high winds you may need to use additional lag bolts to better secure the roof-to-wall unions.

5. Wheel in the grill, fire it up and let it rain!

Arbor

Every well-tended garden needs the graceful curves of a shady, flower-covered arbor. This one is easily built of thin strips cut from 2 x 4s. Overall dimensions are 36 x 39 x 80 inches.

Figure A   1 square = 1 inch   **Figure B**

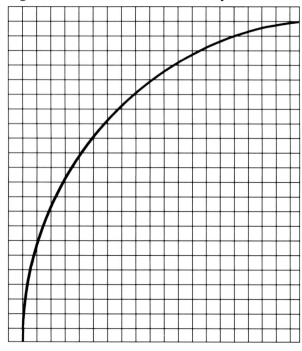

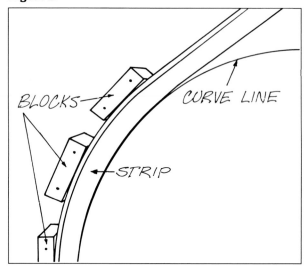

Materials

The lattice is made by ripping ⅛ x 1½-inch strips from larger stock. Four 12-foot lengths of standard white pine 2 x 4 will provide enough lattice to complete all of the required work. Avoid using yellow pine or fir, because these woods are stiffer and more likely to break when bent.

In addition to the lumber for the lattice, you'll need four 12-foot lengths of standard white pine 2 x 4 to build the frame arches.

A large, flat surface on which to set up a form jig. An old door or large sheet of plywood will work just fine. You'll also need two 5-foot lengths and several smaller scrap pieces of 2 x 2 to use as braces on the form jig.

Approximately 20 linear feet of waxed paper, also to use on the form jig

No. 17 wire brads, each ¾-inch long, or staple gun and ½-inch staples

No. 6 gauge wood screws, each 2 inches long

Waterproof wood glue, and exterior wood stain and sealer or exterior paint

The arbor consists of two identical laminated frame arches joined by two solid wood pieces at the bottom, and covered with two layers of lattice. We suggest that you begin by ripping all but one of the 2 x 4s into ⅛-inch-thick strips, which will provide enough stock for both the arches and lattice work.

Building the Frame

The arches of the arbor frame each consist of eleven strips that are bent, glued, and clamped around a curve. A scale drawing for one-half of the curve is provided in **Figure A**.

1. To set up the form jig, enlarge the drawing (**Figure A**) and transfer the curve to the plywood or door that you're using as a form jig. Nail the two 5-foot lengths of 2 x 4 parallel to each other at the lower ends of the curve.

2. The first strip you bend will be the outermost strip of the arch. To begin, clamp one 12-foot strip to the left-hand 2 x 2 on the form jig. Following the curve line, bend the first few inches of the strip, and nail a block of 2 x 2 along the outer edge of the arch (**Figure B**). Clamp the strip to the block to hold it in place along the curve. Bend the next few inches of the strip along the curve line, nail another block in place, and clamp. Repeat this procedure until you reach the long 2 x 2 on the right-hand side of the arch (**Figure C**).

Figure C
Figure D

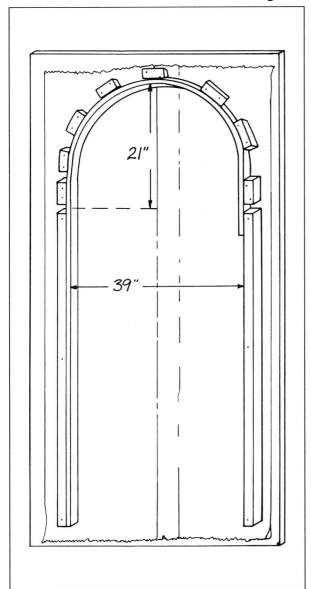

21"

39"

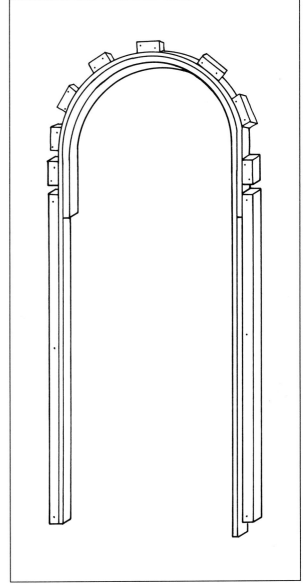

3. Following the glue manufacturer's directions, apply glue to another strip, or to both the curved strip and next strip. To add the next strip, begin from the right-hand side of the jig. Loosen the clamps slightly, and bend the strip around the inside of the first one, placing the glued sides together, as shown in **Figure D**. Tighten the clamps.

4. Cut a short strip to fit at the end of each curved strip, so that the entire arch is two strips thick. Glue and clamp the short strips to the curved strips, as shown in **Figure E**. You don't need to make all the strips come out even – we just let them run wild, and cut them off later. Allow the glue between the strips to set, according to manufacturer's directions.

Figure E

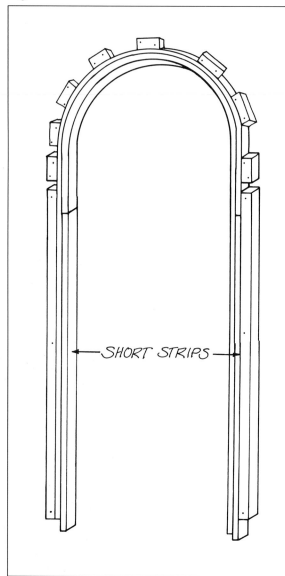

SHORT STRIPS

Figure F

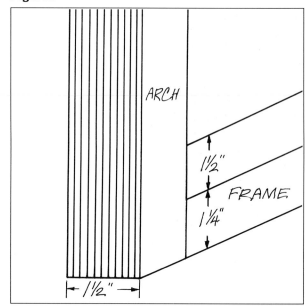

ARCH

1½"

FRAME

1¼"

1½"

6. Cut the strips at each end of the arch so that they are even. Remove the arch from the jig, and sand off any excess glue.

7. Repeat the procedures described in this section to make an identical arch.

8. Cut two frame connectors from 2 x 4, each 1¼ x 1½ x 33 inches. Attach one frame connector to each end of an arch, as shown in **Figure F**. Secure with glue, and insert two screws through the arch into each connector. Attach the remaining arch to the opposite end of each frame connector in the same manner.

Attaching the Latticework

1. Begin assembling the latticework on the outside of the right-hand front corner of the frame, as shown in **Figure G**. Miter the ends of one lattice strip to fit close to the corner, at a 45-degree angle to the horizontal and vertical pieces of the support frame, and tack it in place. Miter and add a second lattice strip, allowing a 1½-inch space between the first and second strips. An easy way to achieve even spacing is to use an extra lattice strip as a spacer. Continue adding lattice strips in this manner. As you near the top, you'll have to bend the strips along the curve (**Figure H**). Continue to add strips until you reach the left-hand rear corner.

5. Loosen the clamps slightly, and bend and glue another strip around the inside of the arch, beginning again from the left-hand side. Continue adding strips in this manner, alternately bending the strips from the right and left sides, until you have an eleven-strip-thick sandwich. Clamp the arch together tightly, using a clamp every few inches around the curve, and allow the assembly to dry thoroughly.

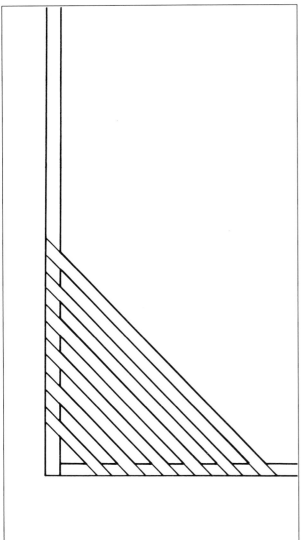

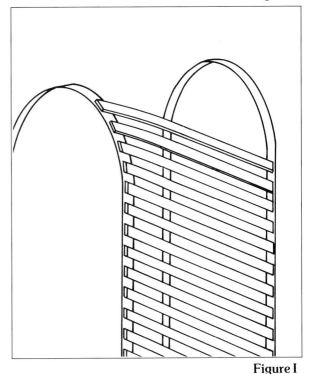

Figure I

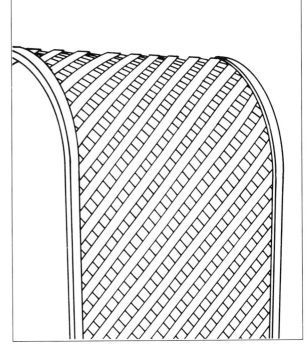

2. Repeat the procedures in step 1 to create a second lattice layer on top of the first one. This time, begin in the left front corner and work to the right rear corner, so that the strips of the second layer are at a 90-degree angle to those of the first layer. For a neater appearance, you can glue and tack the lattice strips together at the points where they cross over each other, but do so sparingly, or you'll split the strips.

3. Tack a lattice strip over the latticework along each arch, as shown in **Figure I**.

Wishing Well

Once upon a time, when every village had a well at its center, it was believed that spirits took up residence there. Of course the better looking your well, the better the quality of occupant you got. Drop a little loose change in, make a wish, and hope the spirit of the well looked kindly upon having coins dropped on its head.

You're sure to draw a class tenant with this wishing well project. You can make this rustic lawn decoration from inexpensive waferwood, some shingles, and 2 x 4's. The base is a 35-inch-wide hexagon, 38 inches tall. The roof peak is just over 6 feet tall. Go ahead, make a wish come true!

Materials

18 linear feet of pine 2 x 2 (Or you can use a 9-foot length of 2 x 4 ripped in half.)

31 linear feet of pine 2 x 4

33 square feet of ½-inch waferwood

41-inch length of ¾-inch-diameter wooden dowel rod

A few inches of 1-inch diameter wooden dowel rod for washers

Two bundles of flat cedar shingles

3d or 4d finishing nails

⁹⁄₁₆-inch staples or roofing nails

Six No. 6 gauge flathead wood screws 1½ inches long, and two 1 inch long

Waterproofing wood sealer, wood stain, carpenter's wood glue

Cutting the Wood

1. The pieces listed below are cut from ½-inch waferwood. Cut and label each piece.

Quantity	Part	Dimensions
6	Side	15 x 36 inches
2	Roof	21 x 33 inches

2. The pieces listed below are lengths of 2 x 4 pine. Cut and label each piece.

Quantity	Part	Length
2	Support	72 inches
4	Rafter	18¼ inches
4	Brace	13 inches
6	Trim	16⅝ inches

3. The pieces listed below are lengths of 2 x 2 pine. Cut and label each piece.

Quantity	Part	Length
6	Corner	36 inches

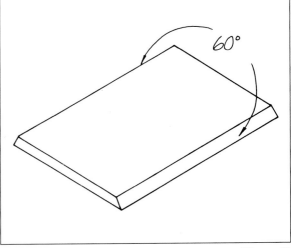

Figure A

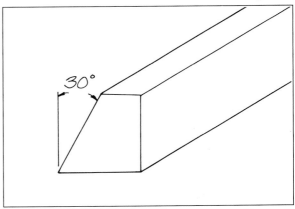

Figure B

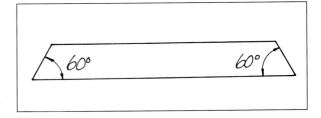

Figure C

4. Bevel both long edges of each Side piece at a 60-degree angle as shown in **Figure A**.

5. Bevel one long edge of each Corner piece at a 30-degree angle as shown in **Figure B**.

6. Miter both ends of each Trim piece at a 60-degree angle as shown in **Figure C**.

Figure D

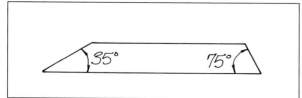

Figure E

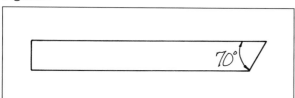

Figure F

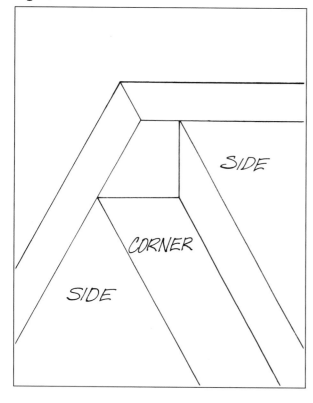

7. Miter one end of each Brace piece at a 35-degree angle, and the opposite end at a 75-degree angle as shown in **Figure D**.

8. Miter one end of each Rafter at a 70-degree angle as shown in **Figure E**. Do not miter the opposite end.

Figure G

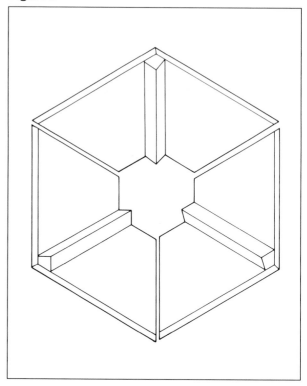

Assembly

We've divided the assembly into two sections, the base and the roof. In the final assembly, you'll put the roof on the base, then add the shingles, trim, and hand crank (spirits optional).

Assembling the Base

1. It's easiest to build the well base in three sections (each section composed of two Sides and one Corner piece). Attach two Side pieces by glueing the beveled edges together; secure the joint by nailing through the Sides into the beveled edges of a Corner piece (refer to **Figure F**).

2. Follow the procedures in step 1 to build two more identical sections, using all the remaining Side pieces, and two of the remaining Corner pieces.

3. To finish the base, join the three sections using the remaining Corner pieces as shown in **Figure G**. Glue and nail each joint.

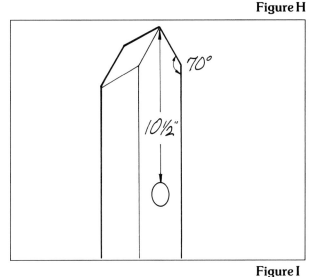

Figure I

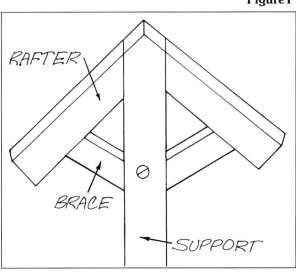

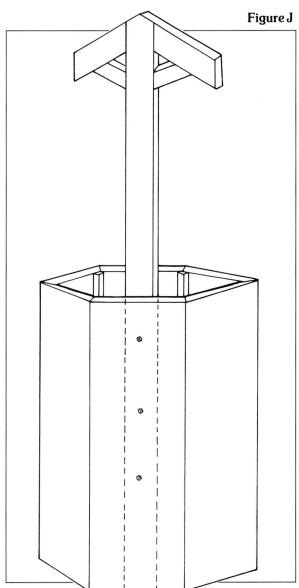

Assembling the Roof Frame

1. Cut the upper end of each Support piece into a peak as shown in **Figure H**. Center and drill a $^{13}/_{16}$-inch-diameter hole $10\frac{1}{2}$ inches from the peak end of each Support piece.

2. The frame is constructed one side at a time. Attach the Rafter and Brace pieces to the Support piece as shown in **Figure I**, toenailing the joints. The upper edge of each Rafter should be flush with the mitered corner of the Support piece, as shown.

Final Assembly

1. To attach the roof frame to the well base, center one Support piece on the inner surface of one Side piece of the base. Secure it with glue and three $1\frac{1}{2}$-inch screws (**Figure J**). The lower ends of the Support and Side pieces should be flush.

2. Attach the remaining Support piece to the opposite Side of the well base, securing with glue and screws.

Figure K

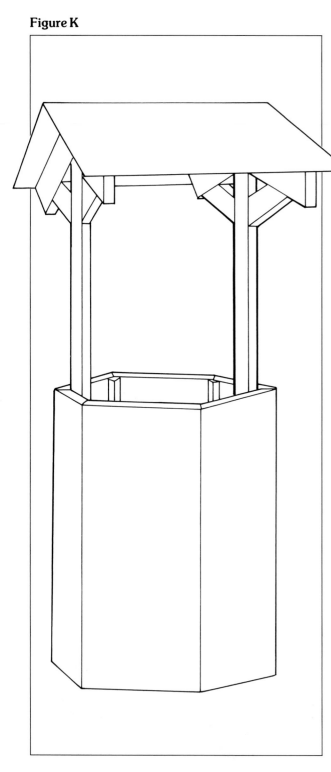

Figure L

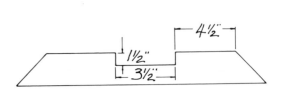

Figure M

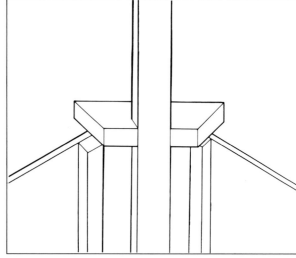

3. Glue and nail the Roof pieces to the rafters, butting their upper edges at the peak of the roof (**Figure K**). We chose not to bevel the Roof piece edges (we'd had enough beveling by this time!) and the slight gap at the peak of the roof can be covered by shingles.

4. The Trim is attached to the upper edge of the base, and supported by the inside Corner pieces. Modify two of the trim pieces to fit around the Support pieces as shown in **Figure L**. Cut a 1½ x 3½-inch notch, centered on the shorter edge of the board.

5. Attach each of the notched Trim pieces to the upper edges of the base where the roof supports are connected (**Figure M**). The inner edge of the Trim piece should now be flush with the inner edge of a Corner piece. Secure the joints by nailing through the Trim piece into the ends of the Corner pieces.

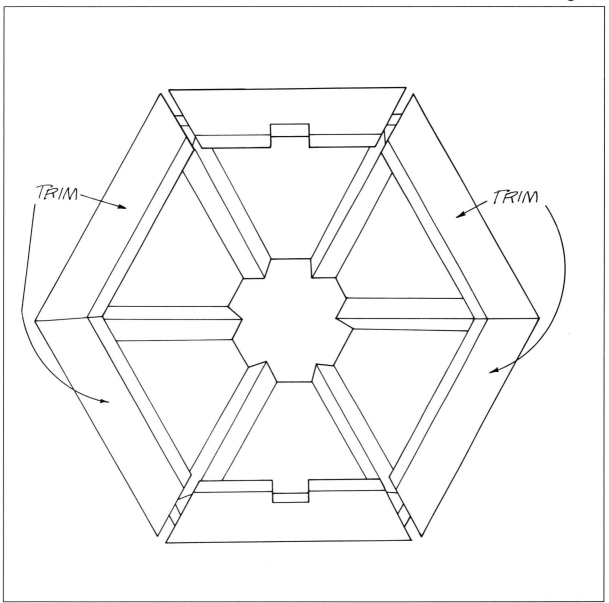

TRIM

TRIM

6. Attach the remaining Trim pieces in the same manner, matching the mitered ends around the well base (**Figure N**). For extra strength, we toenailed each Trim piece joint.

7. Attach the shingles starting at the lower end of the base, overlapping them approximately eight inches.

With that amount of overlap, we were able to put five rows on each side (**Figure O**). We used a staple gun with ⁹⁄₁₆-inch staples. Roofing nails will work just as well, but the ends will protrude on the inside of the well base. For better weatherproofing, the shingle edges on each row should overlap the edges of the row under-

Figure O

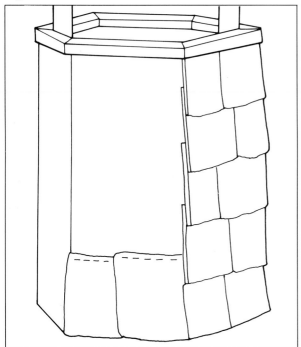

Figure P

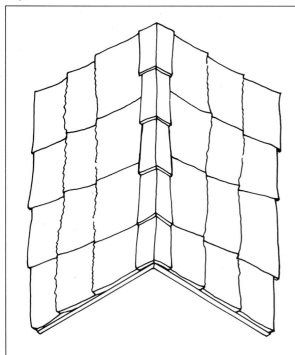

Figure Q

Figure R

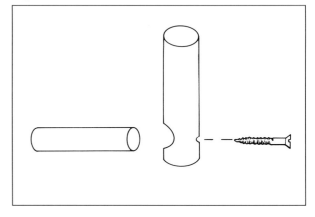

neath it (**Figure O**). You'll need to trim the shingles to different widths to allow for the overlap.

8. Shingle the roof in the same way as the sides, starting at each lower edge and working to the peak. To cover the peak, cut several 2-inch-wide shingle strips and overlap them along the upper edge of each Roof piece as shown in **Figure P**.

Assembling the Hand Crank

The hand crank is assembled in two sections, the shaft and the crank handle.

1. Cut a 28-inch length of the wooden dowel rod to make the shaft. Drill a shallow ¾-inch-diameter socket ¾ inch from one end (**Figure Q**). Drill a screw hole through the center of the socket, enlarging it on the opposite side so you can countersink a screw.

2. To make a handle, cut a 7¼-inch length of dowel rod and drill a shallow ¾-inch-diameter socket ¾ inch from one end. Drill and enlarge a screw hole in this socket the same way you did in step 1. Insert one end of the remaining piece of dowel rod into the socket, securing it with glue and a 1-inch screw from the opposite side (**Figure R**).

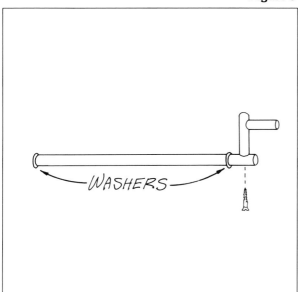

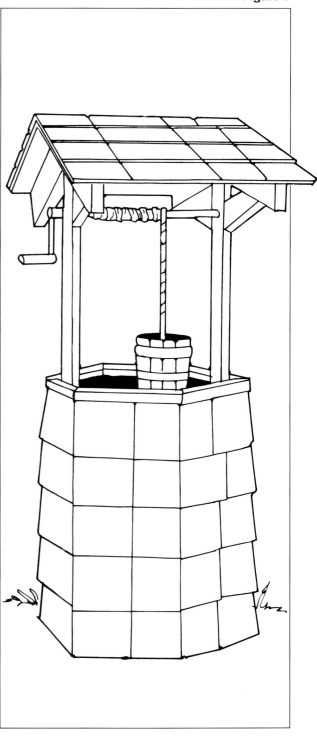

3. Insert the assembled handle into the socket of the shaft, and secure it with glue and a 1-inch screw from the opposite side (**Figure S**).

4. Make a pair of wooden washers to hold the hand crank shaft in place by drilling a ¾-inch-diameter hole into the center of a 1-inch diameter dowel rod. Slice off two ¼-inch pieces to make the washers.

5. To install the hand crank, slip one washer on the end of the shaft and slide it all the way down to the handle. Slide the shaft into one hole in one of the roof support pieces, continuing through the hole in the opposite support. Glue the remaining washer on the tip of the shaft that protrudes through the support. Glue the washer on the handle end of the crank so the crank will turn easily.

For an authentic touch, add a rope and a wooden bucket as in **Figure T.** (The older and more weathered the better!)

Finishing

Stain or paint the wishing well, or leave it natural. We opted to stain only the exposed 2 x 4 pieces, leaving the shingles to age naturally. If the finished piece will be exposed to harsh weather conditions, you may wish to apply a waterproof finish to avoid deterioration.

Park Bench

Create your own park setting for this handsome redwood bench. It will seat three but you might like to spend an occasional morning hogging it all to yourself, with a bag of popcorn to share with the birds. Just like a real city park, without the city! Overall dimensions are 49 x 20 x 37 inches. We made it without armrests but have included instructions for adding them if you want to.

Materials

For the bench:
18 linear feet of 2 x 6 redwood
33 linear feet of 1 x 8 redwood
27 linear feet of 1 x 2 redwood
Two ¼ x 3½ roundhead stove bolts, each with two 1¼-inch-long tight-joint fasteners (which are rectangular flat nuts)
Eight No. 18 gauge, 3½ or 4-inch-long flathead wood screws
No. 12 gauge, 2½-inch-long flathead wood screws
No. 6 gauge, 1½-inch-long flathead wood screws
4d finishing nails

For the arms:
You can add any type of arms you like. Many lumberyards, hardware dealers, and home improvement centers carry wrought iron arm hardware that can be attached with screws, and that's that. If you prefer to make wooden arms like those illustrated in **Figure O**, purchase a 6-foot length of redwood 2 x 4 in addition to the lumber for the bench itself.

Our park bench consists of two identical end sections connected by seat and back slats and by a 2 x 6 brace between the back legs. Each end section has a thick outer layer and a thinner inner layer, to which slat supports are attached. The outer layer is composed of three parts connected by large dovetail joints. We recommend that you take special care in sealing the bench, because the dovetails will tend to swell and crack if it gets wet too often.

Cutting the Parts

1. Cut the parts listed below from redwood 2 x 6 and label each with its identifying code. All of the parts will be modified according to instructions provided in subsequent steps, but for now cut them to the overall dimensions given here.

Code	Length	Quantity
A	38 inches	2
B	19 inches	2
C	18 inches	2
D	4 inches	1
E	44¼ inches	1

1 square = 1 inch   **Figure A**

A

DRILL ¼" DIA. HOLE

2. The outer layer of each end section is composed of one A, one B, one C, and one D piece (shown in **Figure G**). The A piece will serve as the back leg and must be modified as shown in the scale drawing, **Figure A**. Enlarge the drawing to make a full-size pattern and use it as a guide to modify both A pieces, one for each end section. In addition to cutting the contours and

Figure B   1 square = 1 inch   **Figure C**

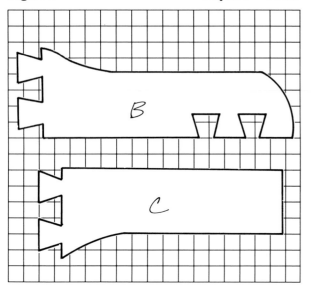

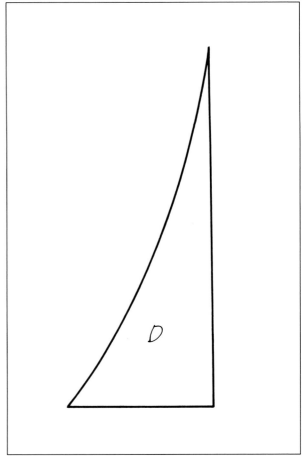

dovetails as shown, drill a ¼-inch-diameter hole through each leg where indicated on the drawing, to accommodate the bolt that connects the leg to the horizontal brace. Choose one side of each leg as the outer side (they must be opposite sides), and enlarge the hole on that side, making it 1½ inches in diameter to a depth of 1 inch. This recess will accommodate the bolt head, which will be covered with a plug.

3. Scale drawings for the seat support B and front leg C are provided in **Figure B**. Enlarge the drawings to make a full-size pattern for each piece and use them to modify both B pieces and both C pieces.

4. A full-size pattern for the corner trim D is provided in **Figure C**. Trace the drawing and use your tracing as a guide to cut two corner trims from the D piece that you cut in step 1. Label each piece D.

5. The E piece will serve as the brace that connects the back legs of the two end sections. (You can see this assembly in **Figure K**). We ripped the brace to a width of 4 inches, because we felt that it looked too heavy, but it's not absolutely necessary. It is necessary to do a bit of drilling on this piece, to accommodate the bolts that will hold it in place. First, drill a ¼-inch-diameter socket, 1½ inches deep, straight into one end of the board at the exact center. Drill in as straight a line as is humanly (or mechanically) possible. Choose one side

of the board as the back and drill into this side a 1½-inch-diameter socket, 1 inch deep, placing the center of the socket 2 inches from the drilled end of the board and midway between the upper and lower edges. This socket will intersect the first one. Drill the opposite end of the board in the same manner.

6. Cut the parts listed below from 1 x 8 redwood and label each with its identifying code.

Code	Length	Quantity
F	38 inches	2
G	20 inches	2
H	4 inches	2
I	6 inches	2
J	44¼ inches	5

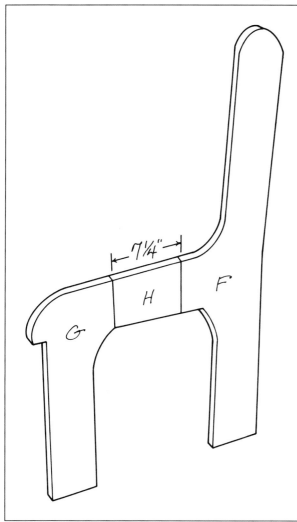

7. As we said earlier, each end section has a thin lining layer in addition to the thick outer layer for which you have already contoured the parts. The lining layer is the same overall shape as the assembled outer layer, but the parts are simply edge-glued and attached to the outer layer – you won't have to cut any more dovetails! Each lining layer consists of one F, one G, and one H piece, contoured to match the outer layer as shown in **Figure D**. The easiest way to contour these pieces is to place them side by side on a flat surface, temporarily assemble the outer layer of one end section, place the

outer layer on top of the aligned F, G, and H pieces, and trace around the outer edge. Then simply cut the contours. Mark the position of the ¼-inch-diameter hole in the back leg, and drill a matching hole through the F piece. Contour both F, both G, and both H pieces in this manner.

8. The I pieces will serve as slat supports. (One slat-support assembly is shown in **Figure H**.) Enlarge the scale drawing for the I piece provided in **Figure E**, and use the pattern to contour both I pieces.

9. The seat and back slats are ripped from the J pieces. You'll need a total of thirteen slats, each 2 inches wide and 44¼ inches long.

Figure F

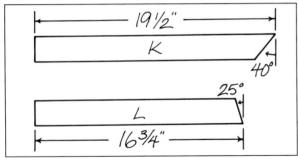

10. Cut the parts listed below from redwood 1 x 2 and label each with its code.

Code	Length	Quantity
K	20 inches	2
L	17 inches	2
M	42¾ inches	5

11. The K and L pieces will serve as back- and seat-slat supports respectively. Cutting diagrams for both pieces are provided in **Figure F**. Miter one end of each K piece at a 40-degree angle, and trim the board to a length of 19½ inches, measuring along the long edge. Miter one end of each L piece at a 25-degree angle and trim the board to 16¾ inches along the long edge.

Assembly

1. Glue together the four pieces that form the outer layer of one end section as shown in **Figure G**. Use the longest screws to secure the dovetail joints, inserting one down through the B piece into each joint with the C piece, and inserting one horizontally through the A piece into each joint with the B piece. Secure the D piece with a few finishing nails.

2. Assemble an identical end section in the same manner, using the remaining A, B, C and D pieces.

3. Glue together an F, G, and H piece to form the lining layer of one end section. Glue the lining assembly to the inside of one outer layer (remember that the hole in the back leg of the outer layer is enlarged on the outside, not on the inside surface). Secure the layers by driving finishing nails through the lining layer into the outer layer. Glue and nail together the remaining lining and outer layers in the same manner.

Figure G

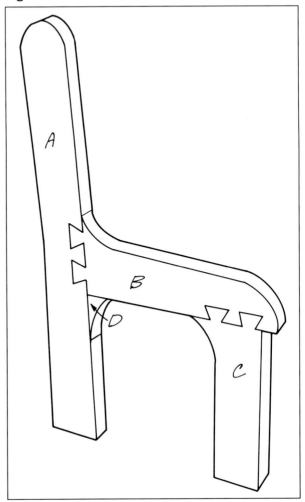

4. Glue three slat supports (K, L, and I pieces) to the lining layer of one end section as shown in **Figure H**. Note the placement dimensions provided in the drawing. The L piece should just clear the curve at the back leg, and the I piece should be turned so the longer edge lies along the L piece. Secure the supports by inserting 2½-inch screws through them, into the end section. Assemble and attach the remaining slat supports to the other end section in the same manner.

5. Bolt the horizontal brace E to one end section, using one of the stove bolts as shown in **Figure I**. Be sure that the brace is turned so that the side with the large sockets faces the back. Attach the opposite end

Figure H

Figure I

Figure J

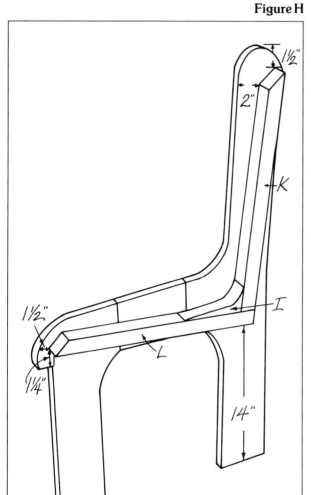

of the brace to the other end section in the same manner and tighten the bolts. Cut four redwood plugs to cover the sockets.

6. The M pieces will serve as additional supports for the seat slats, to keep them from sagging. They are attached between the L and I supports on the two end sections as shown in **Figure J**, which is a cross-section diagram indicating where the ends of the M supports and J slats should be placed. Glue the M supports in place and secure each one by angling a screw up through the lower edge, into the L or I piece.

PARK BENCH

49

Figure K

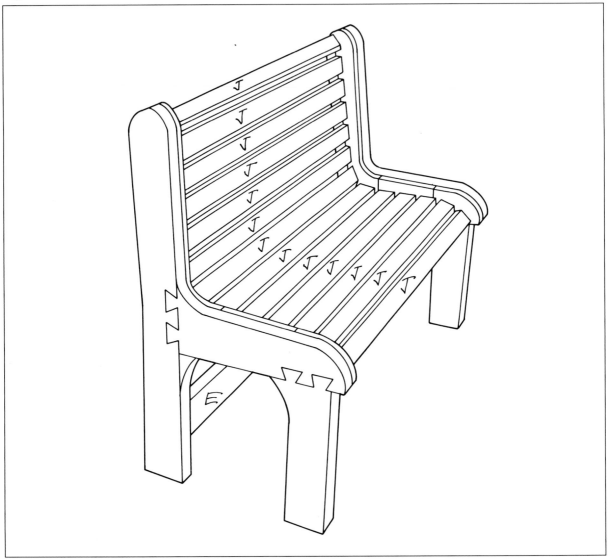

Figure L

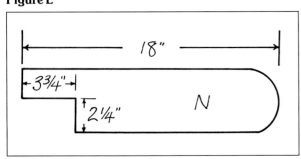

Figure M

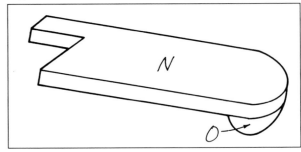

7. The assembled bench is shown in **Figure K**. Glue the slats J between the end sections, resting on the supports as shown in **Figure J**. There is a space of approximately ¾ inch between each two slats. Secure each end of each slat by inserting two of the shorter screws down through the slat into the support. For the angled front slat, secure each end with only one screw.

Adding Arms

1. Cut the parts listed below from redwood 2 x 4 and label each with its identifying code.

Code	Length	Quantity
N	18 inches	2
O	3 inches	2
P	10 inches	2

2. The N pieces will serve as the armrests. A cutting diagram is provided in **Figure L**. Cut the notch as shown and round off the three designated corners of each N piece.

3. The O pieces serve as decorative additions to the armrests, as shown in **Figure M**. Glue an O piece to the bottom of one contoured N armrest and secure it by inserting a couple of screws up through the bottom. Round off the corners to match. Then round off the entire front end of the assembly to create a smooth line, and shape the back lower edge of the O piece to finish. Attach the remaining O piece to the other armrest and shape in the same manner.

4. The P pieces will serve as armrest supports. A cutting diagram is provided in **Figure N**. Cut a notch in each P piece as shown.

5. Each arm is assembled and attached to the bench as shown in **Figure O**. Glue the support P to the seat and secure by inserting two long screws through the lower extension of the support into the end section. Recess the screws and cover the holes with plugs. Place the armrest on top, with the notch against the back of the end section, and glue it to the support and to the bench back. Secure it with screws inserted down through the armrest into the support, and horizontally through the armrest into the bench back. Attach the remaining arm assembly in the same manner.

Figure N

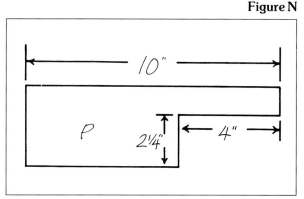

Figure O

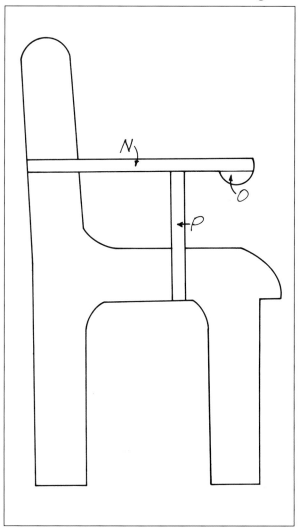

Purple Martin Mission

House thirty-two martin families in this 28 x 28 x 39-inch mission!

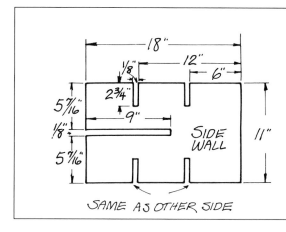

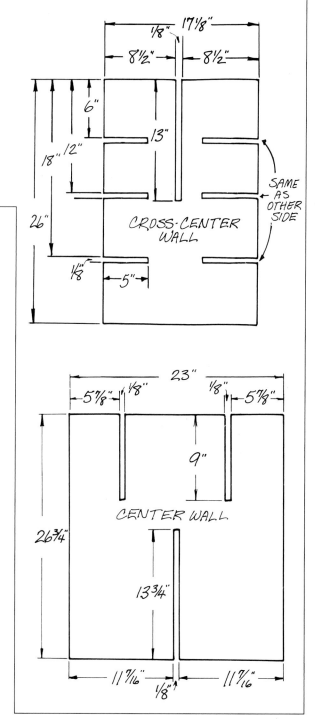

Materials

7 square feet of ¾-inch exterior plywood

15 square feet of ½-inch exterior plywood

16 square feet of ¼-inch exterior plywood

21 square feet of ⅛-inch exterior plywood or tempered formica for the interior walls. You can substitute ¼-inch plywood if you prefer. We opted for the formica to cut down on the weight of the mission.

23 square feet of ⅛-inch oak for the shingles and trim

7 feet of 1½-inch wooden dowel or closet rod

3 feet of ½-inch wooden dowel rod

16 feet of ¼-inch wooden dowel rod

Building the Inner Structure

The inner structure consists of interior walls and floors connected to a base. Because martin houses should be mounted 15 to 20 feet above ground on a pole, we installed a simple housing underneath the base that will accommodate a 3½-inch-diameter pole. You may wish to modify the housing if you have a different size pole.

1. There are four interior walls which are connected by interlocking slots. Cut the following rectangles from ⅛-inch plywood or formica, or from ¼-inch plywood: one Center Wall, 23 x 26¾ inches; one Cross-Center Wall, 17⅛ x 26 inches; and two Side Walls, each 11 x 18 inches.

2. Cut the slots in each wall as shown in **Figure A**. If you are using ¼-inch stock, widen the slots to ¼ inch.

Figure B

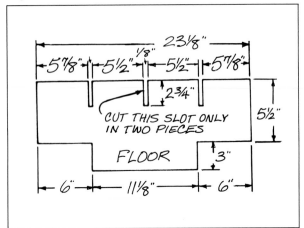

Figure D

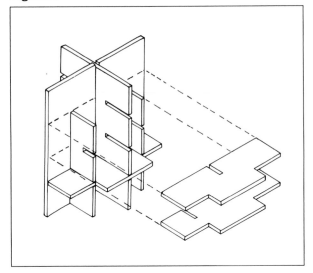

Figure C

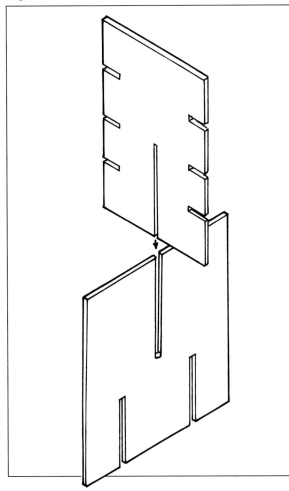

3. The interior floors are also interlocked with the walls. There are six interior Floor pieces, as shown in **Figure B**. Cut all the slots, as shown, in four Floor pieces; cut the center slot only in the remaining pieces.

4. Begin the assembly by sliding the Cross-Center Wall down into the center slot in the Center Wall as shown in **Figure C**. Then slide the two Side Walls into the remaining slots in the Center Wall, from the bottom up this time.

5. Now add the Floors, three on each side of the Center Wall, by sliding them into the appropriate slots in the Cross-Center and Side Walls (**Figure D**). The top Floor slides into the upper slot in the Cross-Center Wall, but it simply rests on top of the Side Walls.

6. Test the strength of the floors by pressing down on them in several places. If some spots are too springy, you may wish to glue support blocks underneath them, even though a bird family doesn't weigh very much.

7. Cut the Base from ¾-inch plywood, following the cutting diagram given in **Figure E**.

8. The pole housing consists of four pieces, two Sides and two Ends, all of which are cut from ¾-inch plywood. A scale drawing of the contoured Side is provided in **Figure F**. The Ends are rectangles, each 3¾ x 4½ inches. Cut the four pieces and assemble them as shown in **Figure G**, then attach the housing to the bottom of the mission Base in the center.

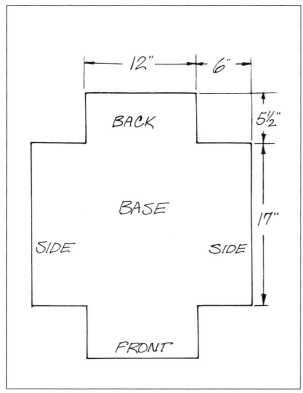

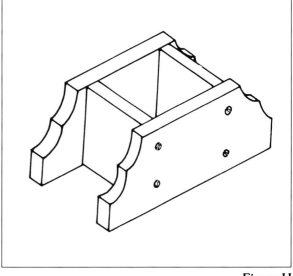

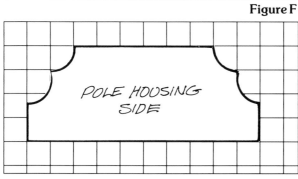

9. The interior wall-and-floor structure can be attached to the base in one of two ways. Either way, the finished assembly is shown in **Figure H**. The simplest method is to stand the interior structure in place and support it with glue blocks glued and nailed to the base and the bottom edges of the walls. The exterior walls of the mission will provide additional support. To make it stronger, you can cut dadoes in the base to accommodate the four walls, and then add the glue blocks.

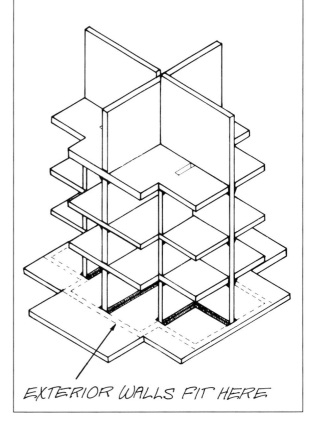

Figure I

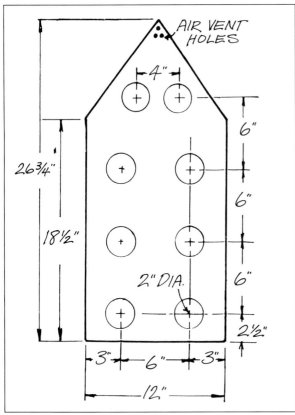

Building the Exterior Structure

This birdhouse is built in an x-shape, as you can see by the outline of the base. There are twelve exterior walls: four wide walls which form the front, back, and sides of the mission; and eight narrower ones which fit together between the wider ones to form the corners. All of the exterior walls are cut from ½-inch plywood.

1. A cutting diagram for the four wide walls is provided in **Figure I**. Cut two of the walls exactly as shown; these will be the Front and Back Walls. For the remaining two Side Walls cut only the upper two entrance holes; do not cut the six lower entrance holes.

2. On the Front and Back Walls only, cut a ¼ x ¼-inch rabbet on the lower front edge to accommodate the plywood porch, which will be added later.

3. Cut four Corner Walls (for the front and back of the mission), each 3 x 18 inches.

4. Glue and nail two of these Corner Walls to the Front Wall, and two to the Back Wall, butting the pieces as shown in **Figure J**. All bottom edges should be even.

5. Cut four Side Corner Walls (for the sides of the mission), each 6 x 18 inches, and cut three entrance holes in each, as shown in **Figure K**.

6. Glue and nail two of these Side Corner Walls to each wide Side Wall, butting the pieces as you did the previous assemblies (**Figure J**). All bottom edges should be even.

7. Each entrance hole has a Perch below it. All Perches are cut from ¼-inch plywood. Cut eight Double Perches, each 2 x 11 inches, for the wide walls. Cut eight Single Perches, each 2 x 5½ inches, for the narrow walls. To support the Perches, cut thirty-two triangular Braces from ¾-inch plywood. Each should be a right triangle with two 1-inch-long sides.

8. The Double Perches are attached to the Front, Back, and Side Walls on the outside (**Figure L**). Place each Perch 1¼ inches below the bottom of the two entrance holes that it serves. Support each Perch with two Braces underneath. The Single Perches are attached to the Side Corner Walls in the same manner.

9. It's a good idea to add a railing around each Perch to provide a twig-like foothold for your feathered friends, and to keep the baby birds from taking a long

Figure J

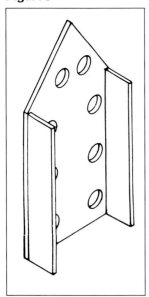

Figure K

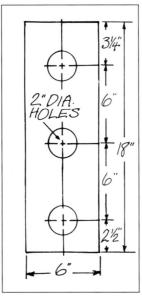

Figure L **Figure M**

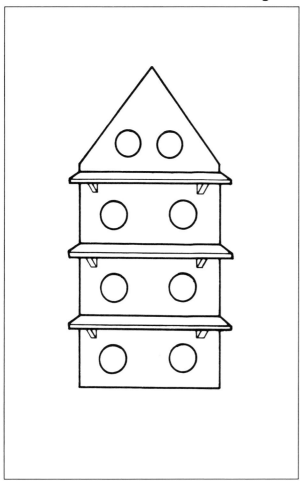

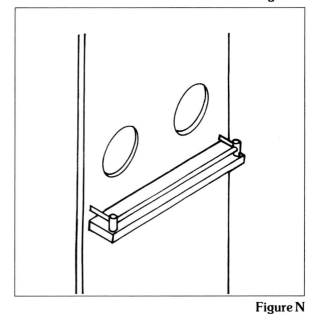

nose dive the first time they venture out of their apartments. We used a simple dowel assembly as shown in **Figure M**. For each Double Perch, you'll need two 1-inch lengths of ½-inch dowel to serve as Posts. In addition, cut two 2-inch lengths of ¼-inch dowel and one 11-inch length of ¼-inch dowel to serve as Rails. We drilled sockets into the Perch to accommodate the Posts, and additional sockets into the Posts and walls to accommodate the Rails. For each Single Perch, cut the same size Posts and the same size short Rails. The one longer Rail for each Single Perch need only be 5½ inches long.

10. Assemble the four sections of the mission, butting the walls together as shown in **Figure N**.

Figure O

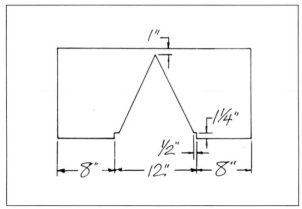

Figure P

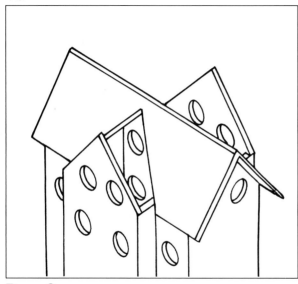

Figure Q

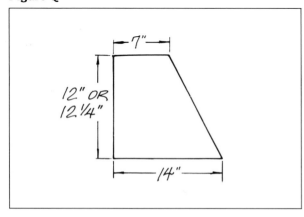

The Roof, Cupola, and Porches

The mission has a plywood roof that is covered with shingles. The roof sections are cut and attached to the walls, the cupola is added, and then the shingles are cut and attached. The porches are added last.

1. The mission roof is cut from ¼-inch plywood in six parts: two long ones and four shorter ones. The long roof pieces extend from side to side, and the shorter pieces cover the front and back sections. Begin by cutting the two long roof pieces: one 12 x 28 inches, and one 12¼ x 28 inches. Refer to **Figure O** as you cut the triangular contour in each of these pieces.

2. Attach the two long roof pieces to the top edges of the mission walls, extending across the side sections (**Figure P**). The wider piece should overlap the narrower piece at the peak of the roof.

3. A cutting diagram for the shorter roof pieces is provided in **Figure Q**. Cut two pieces 12 inches wide and two pieces 12¼ inches wide.

4. Attach two of these pieces over the front mission section, and the remaining two over the back section (**Figure R**). Use one wider and one narrower piece for each section, lapping them at the peak as you did for the long roof pieces.

5. Martins are notoriously unfond of wet quarters, so it's a good idea to caulk or otherwise seal the roof joints. But these birds are also unhappy with a home that is too hot (can't win for losing), so we drilled a few small ventilation holes near the top of each wall, underneath the eaves.

6. The cupola consists of four walls and a roof. Cutting diagrams for the Front/Back and Side Walls are provided in **Figure S**. Cut two of each type of wall from ¼-inch plywood.

7. Assemble the cupola, placing the Front and Back Walls inside the Side Walls.

8. Cut two Cupola Roof sections from ¼-inch plywood: one 3¾ x 6¾ inches, and one 4 x 6¾ inches. Attach them to the upper edges of the cupola walls, lapping the wider roof section over the edge of the narrower one at the peak.

9. Glue the cupola to the center of the mission roof.

10. The mission and cupola roofs are covered with shingles cut from ⅛-inch oak. We cut the shingles 2¼ inches long, and of varying widths. Attach the shingles

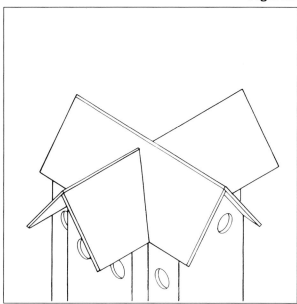

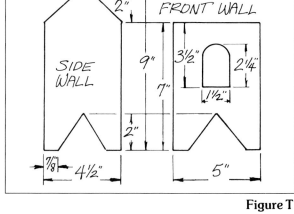

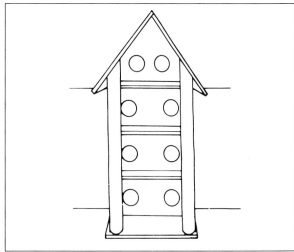

to the roof sections in overlapping horizontal rows, beginning at the bottom. The first row should overhang the plywood roof by about ¼ inch, and each successive row should overlap the row below it by approximately 1 inch.

11. The roof peaks are coverd with trim strips cut from ⅛-inch oak. For each peak, measure the length between the cupola and the end of the roof and then cut two strips to that length: one ⅝ inch wide, and one ½ inch wide. Glue them to the shingles along the sides of the peak, lapping the wider one over the narrower one at the top. Cut and attach trim strips to the cupola and roof peak in the same manner.

12. There are two porches on the mission: one at the back, and one at the front. Cut two Porch Floors from ¼-inch plywood, each 5 x 12 inches. Cut four Porch Columns from 1½-inch dowel or closet rod, each 20 inches long.

13. For the back porch, first insert one long edge of the Porch Floor into the rabbet at the bottom of the Back Wall. Glue and nail it in place. The Columns are cut at an angle at the top to fit between the Porch Floor and the underside of the roof, as shown in **Figure T**. Trim the Columns and glue them in place. Assemble the front porch in the same manner.

Finishing

Paint the entire mission, inside and out (omitting the shingles, of course), using white paint. When you slip the exterior structure over the interior one, remember that it will fit only if it is turned in the right direction.

As a finishing touch, we cut a cross for the top of the cupola. The one that we made was cut from a solid piece of pine using a band saw. We started with a 1½ x 2 x 4-inch block of wood, and made the cross portion ½ inch thick, 3¼ inches tall, and 1⅞ inches wide. The lower ¾ inch of the block was left as a base, and an inverted V-shaped groove was cut into the bottom to accommodate the cupola roof peak.

Pet Shelter

If Snoopy has room for a pool table in his basement, this shelter has room for a pool hall! It's large enough for a good-sized dog, and features a front porch suitable for gourmet bone munching. One side is removable for easy interior cleaning. Overall dimensions: 42 x 47 x 69 inches.

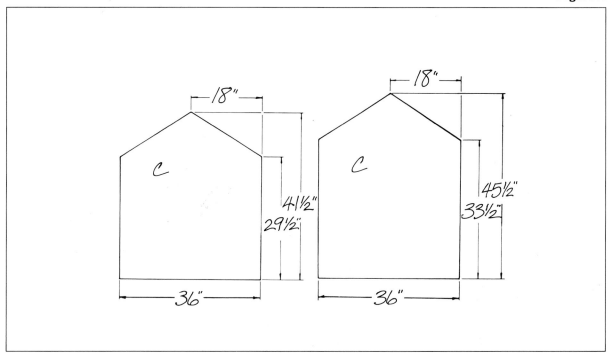

Materials

Two 4 x 8-foot sheets of ½-inch-thick waferwood or exterior plywood

Two 4 x 8-foot sheets of ¼-inch-thick waferwood or exterior plywood

65 linear feet of standard pine or cedar 1 x 4

95 linear feet of standard pine 2 x 4

One-half square of asphalt or wood shingles (enough to cover 25 square feet)

12 linear feet of tar roofing paper, 36 inches wide. (If you can't persuade your dealer to sell you such a small quantity, it's not absolutely necessary.)

No. 6 gauge flathead wood screws, each 2 inches long (if you wish to make one side removable)

8d galvanized nails and waterproof wood glue

½-inch staples or roofing nails

Penetrating oil stain or exterior paint

Cutting the Wood

1. Cut and label the pieces listed at right from waferwood or 2 x 4, as indicated.

Code	Dimensions in inches	Quantity
Cut from waferwood:		
A	½ x 36 x 60	1
B	½ x 24 x 66	2
C	¼ x 36 x 45½	2
D	¼ x 33 x 40	2
E	½ x 13½ x 36	1
Cut from 2 x 4:		
F	1½ x 3½ x 57	3
G	1½ x 3½ x 34½	4
H	1½ x 3½ x 33	1
I	1½ x 3½ x 36	5
J	1½ x 3½ x 21	6
K	1½ x 3½ x 26	4
L	1½ x 1½ x 28	2
M	1½ x 1½ x 11½	2
N	1½ x 1½ x 22½	2
O	1½ x 1½ x 15	12

Figure B

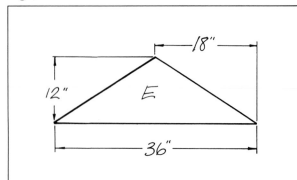

Figure C

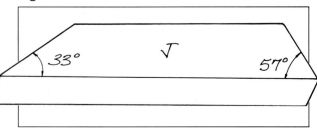

Figure D

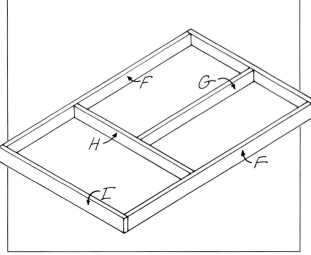

Figure E

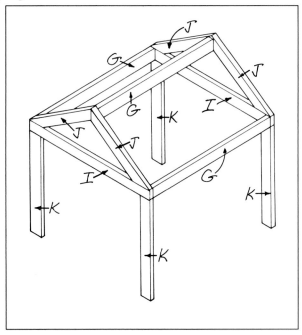

2. The C pieces will serve as the front and back of the shelter, and the E piece will be the porch gable. A cutting diagram for the C pieces is provided in **Figure A**. A cutting diagram for the E piece is provided in **Figure B**. Cut these pieces from the rectangular pieces you cut in step 1.

3. The J pieces will serve as rafters. Miter one end of each J piece at a 33-degree angle, and the opposite end at a 57-degree angle, as shown in **Figure C**.

4. Miter one end of each M and each N piece at a 45-degree angle.

Assembling the Floor

1. The floor support consists of a rectangular frame with inner support pieces. To build the floor support, assemble two F, one G, H, and two I pieces, butting the ends as shown in **Figure D**. Secure the joints with nails.

2. Place the A piece over the assembled floor support, and nail it in place.

The Frame, Sides, and Roof

1. The assembled frame is shown in **Figure E**. To begin, assemble a rectangle, using two G and two I pieces. Nail the K pieces to each corner of the rectangle, then nail on the J pieces as shown. Finally, nail the remaining G piece at the peak formed by the J pieces.

2. Place the assembled frame on the floor section, and secure it by toe-nailing through each K piece into the floor support pieces.

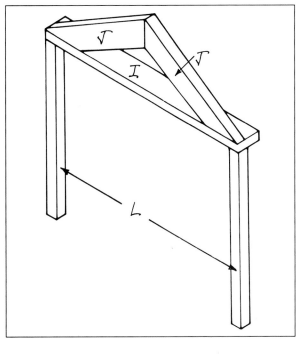

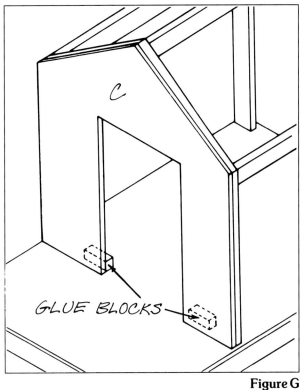

Figure G

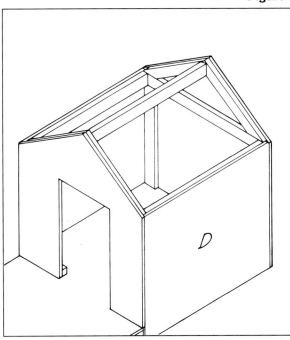

3. Cut a doorway opening in the front C piece. You can determine the size of the doorway by considering the size of your dog. We cut a 16 x 24-inch doorway. Attach the C piece to the front end of the frame. Attach a glue block to the C piece at each side of the doorway, and toe-nail each block into the floor frame, as shown in **Figure F**.

4. Attach the back C piece to the frame in the same manner as you did the front piece. Attach the D pieces to the sides of the frame, butting the ends as shown in **Figure G**. If you wish to make one side removable, tack it to the frame using as few nails as possible, so that you can reinstall it and secure it using screws after the trim pieces are attached.

5. To build the porch frame, attach one L piece to each end of an I piece, butting the ends as shown in **Figure H**. Attach two J pieces to the I piece as shown. Place the frame on the front end of the floor assembly, and toe-nail through each L piece.

6. Attach the B pieces to the top of the frame, butting the upper edges as shown in **Figure I**.

7. Attach the E piece to the porch frame, as shown in **Figure J**.

Figure I

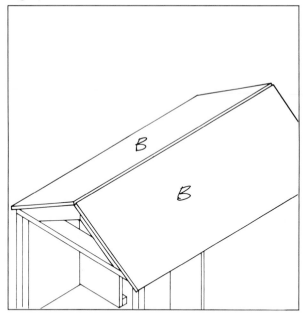

Adding the Trim and Shingles

1. Rip approximately 16 linear feet of the 1 x 4 down to a 2¼-inch width to use for trim to fit around the roof (don't discard the remaining 1¼-inch wide strip). Bevel one long edge of each piece at a 57-degree angle, and miter the ends to fit together neatly at the corners. Install the trim, attaching it to the underside of the B pieces as shown in **Figure K**.

2. Use the remaining 1¼-inch-wide trim (from step 1) to create an additional layer of trim around the roof and front gable. Miter the ends to fit together neatly at the corners, and install this trim over the wider trim you installed in step 1, as shown in **Figure K**.

3. Spread the tarpaper over the roof, and attach the shingles to the roof (B pieces) starting at the lower edge and working to the peak. We used a staple gun with ½-inch staples. Roofing nails will work just as well, but the ends will protrude on the inside of the roof. For better weatherproofing, the shingle edges on reach row should overlap the edges of the row underneath it (**Figure L**). You'll need to trim the shingles to different widths to allow for the overlap. To cover the peak, cut shingle strips and overlap them along the upper edge of each B piece as shown in **Figure L**.

Figure J

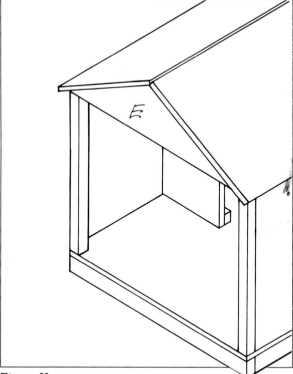

Figure K

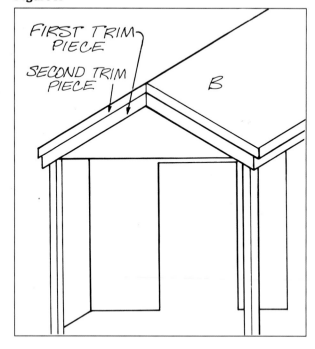

BUILDING OUTDOOR STRUCTURES

Figure L

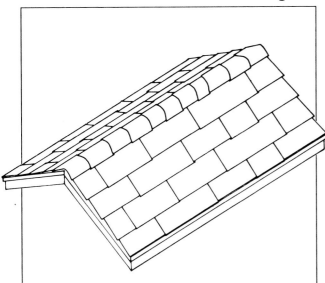

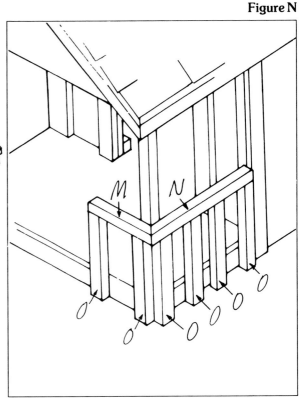

Figure M

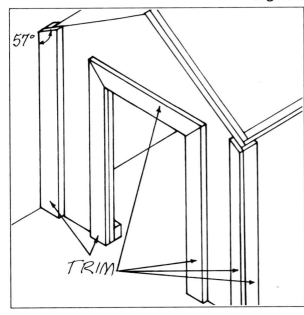

5. Rip from 1 x 4 three 1¼-inch-wide trim pieces to fit around the doorway. Miter the ends to fit together neatly at the corners, and install the trim as shown in **Figure M**.

Final Assembly

1. One side of the assembled porch railing is shown in **Figure N**. To begin, install the O pieces as shown, nailing each one to the floor assembly. Attach each M and N piece along the upper ends of the O pieces, matching the mitered corners as illustrated.

2. To give the shelter a homey touch, we added a window frame on one side, as shown in **Figure O**. Cut the pieces from 1 x 4, miter each piece, and attach to the side using glue and nails. We suggest that you re-move the side (D piece) and place it on a flat surface when you install the window frame. Be sure to remove any nail points extending through the side piece.

3. Stain or paint the shelter, then move the pool table into the basement.

4. Rip an additional 24 linear feet of the 1 x 4 down to a 2¼-inch width to fit over each corner of the shelter. Miter one end of each piece that fits along the front and back at a 57-degree angle. Install the trim as shown in **Figure M**. If you wish to make one side removable, in-stall the trim using screws on that side.

Portable Potting Center

This redwood cabinet can be rolled from garage to yard to patio – wherever a work center is needed. It contains swing-open bins, a drawer, two shelves, and storage space accessible from front or back. We designed it as a potting center, but it makes a handsome storage and work center for the barbecue area as well. Overall dimensions are roughly 3 x 1½ x 5 feet.

Figure A

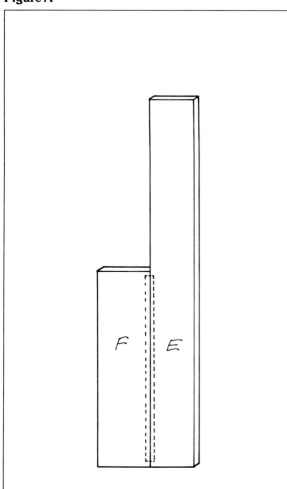

Materials

60 linear feet of redwood 1 x 8

15 linear feet of pine 1 x 12

4 x 8-foot sheet of ¼-inch waferwood or exterior-grade plywood

3-foot length of ¾-inch wooden dowel rod

15-inch length of 1¼-inch wooden closet rod (no waste allowance included)

Three wooden drawer pulls (We used spherical pulls, 1¼ inches in diameter.)

1-foot length of 2 x 4 lumber

Two flat-plate heavy-duty swiveling caster wheels, each 3 inches in diameter

Two 8-inch-diameter lawn mower wheels, each with a washer of corresponding diameter

15-inch length of 1-inch-wide leather strap

Two brass spring-loaded hinges, each about 2 inches long with ¾-inch-wide flanges

Two brass butt hinges, each 4 inches long with ¾-inch-wide flanges

One small suitcase-type latch (This may be more familiar to you as a lunch-box latch.)

One large swiveling plant-hanger

22-inch-long metal axle, ½ inch in diameter, threaded at both ends (Note: If the lawn mower wheels accommodate an axle of a different diameter, purchase an axle of the proper diameter for the wheels.)

Four ¾-inch conduit clips

Galvanized 3d finishing nails

Galvanized tacks

Four No. 9 gauge flathead wood screws, each 1¼ inches long; and six No. 12 gauge flathead wood screws, each 2 inches long

Cutting the Parts

1. Cut from redwood the parts listed here, and label each part with its identifying code. For the parts that are wider than the 1 x 8 stock, you will have to cut two or more boards to the specified length and spline them together to achieve the width.

Code	Dimensions	Quantity
A	7¼ x 32 inches	1
B	7¼ x 30½ inches	1
C	6¾ x 31¼ inches	1
D	6 x 31¼ inches	1
E	7¼ x 58 inches	2
F	8¾ x 31¼ inches	2
G	16⅝ x 32 inches	1
H	6 x 32 inches	1
I	3 x 22¼ inches	3
J	12⅞ x 22 inches	1
K	9⅞ x 22 inches	1
L	3 x 32 inches	1
M	4 x 13 inches	2
N	4 x 12¾ inches	2
O	1¾ x 6 inches	2

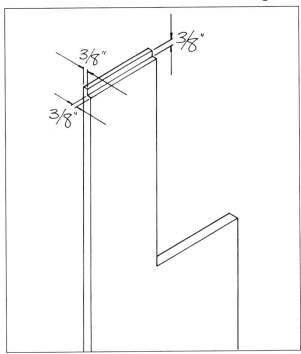

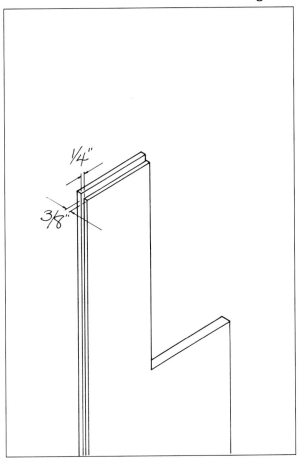

2. Cut from pine the parts listed here, and label each part. Spline the pieces where necessary.

Code	Dimensions	Quantity
P	15½ x 30⅜ inches	1
Q	11 x 17 inches	2
R	7⅞ x 18 inches	2
S	8 x 11 inches	1
T	6 x 7⅞ inches	1
U	5¾ x 14 inches	2
V	¾ x 14 inches	4
W	¾ x 13 inches	1

3. Cut from waferwood or plywood the pieces listed here, and label each part.

Code	Dimensions	Quantity
X	31⅛ x 31⅛ inches	1
Y	26½ x 31⅛ inches	1
Z	14½ x 18 inches	2
AA	12¼ x 13⅛ inches	1
BB	12½ x 18 inches	2

Modifying the Parts

1. The lower portion of the cabinet, which contains the bins, is deeper than the upper portion, which contains the shelves. Each complete cabinet side wall consists of one E and one F piece, as shown in **Figure A**. You should already have splined together two boards to create each F piece. Now spline together one E and one F piece to create one wall. Create a second side wall in the same manner.

2. Cut a ⅜ x ⅜-inch rabbet along what will be the inside top edge of each wall as shown in **Figure B**, to accommodate the cabinet top.

3. Cut a ⅜ x ¼-inch rabbet along what will be the inside back edge of each wall as shown in **Figure C**, to accommodate the waferwood cabinet back.

Figure D

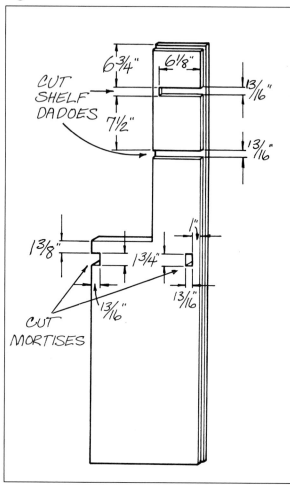

Figure E

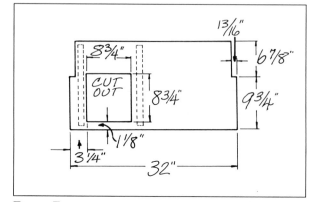

Figure F

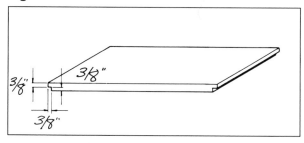

4. Cut two dadoes along what will be the inside surface of each wall as shown in **Figure D**, to accommodate the shelves. Each dado should be ¹³⁄₁₆ inch wide and ⅜ inch deep. The upper dado is stopped, because the upper shelf is narrower to accommodate the hinged door that covers it. The lower dado is a through dado, because the wider shelf extends all the way out to the front of the cabinet and has no door.

5. One wall must be mortised to accommodate the supports that will house the closet-rod handle. Cut two mortises, each ¹³⁄₁₆ x 1¾ inches, in one of the walls as shown in **Figure D**. The upper edges of the two mortises should be even. The front mortise actually is a notch, because it is open at the front as shown.

6. The splined G piece will serve as the counter top and must be notched to accommodate the walls. Modify the G piece on each side as shown in **Figure E**. We cut a hole in the counter top to accommodate a removable plastic container that we use to mix potting soil, etc. The hole we cut is shown in **Figure E**. You may wish to alter the size to fit a container you already have, but the hole should not extend farther than 13 inches from the left edge of the counter top. You may wish to omit the hole altogether. If you cut the hole, we suggest that you reinforce the splined counter top boards on either side. To do this, cut from scrap redwood or pine two support blocks, each 1½ x 15 inches. Glue and nail them underneath the counter top, one on either side of the hole, as shown by the dotted lines in **Figure E**.

7. The A piece will serve as the cabinet top, and is cut to fit the rabbets at the tops of the walls. Cut a ⅜ x ⅜-inch rabbet along what will be the lower edge on each end of the A piece as shown in **Figure F**. Cut an additional ⅜ x ¼-inch rabbet along what will be the lower back edge, to accommodate the waferwood cabinet back.

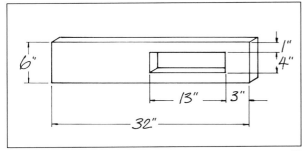

Figure I

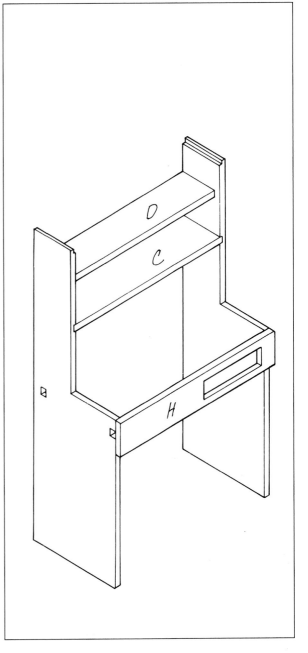

Figure H

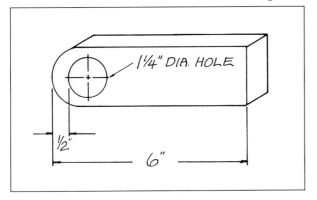

8. The H piece will serve as the upperhorizontal facer of the cabinet front and must be modified to create the drawer opening. Cut a 4 x 13-inch opening in the H piece where indicated in **Figure G**.

9. The O pieces will serve as supports for the closet-rod handle. Round off the corners at one end of one O piece, and drill a 1¼-inch-diameter hole ½ inch from the rounded end, as shown in **Figure H**. Modify the remaining O piece in the same manner, using the first one as a guide so the holes will be aligned precisely.

Assembling the Cabinet

The basic cabinet consists of the two side walls, the counter top, the cabinet top and shelves, a splined pine floor, a waferwood back in two sections, and the facers that form the cabinet front. The bins and drawer are assembled after the basic cabinet is built.

1. Begin by installing the upper shelf (D) and lower shelf (C) between the walls, inserting the ends of the shelves into the dadoes as shown in **Figure I**. Secure the joints with glue and finishing nails.

2. The facers that form the front of the cabinet are added next. Glue and nail the H piece to the front edges of the walls, with all pieces flush at the top (**Figure I**). Cut a ⅞ x 30¼-inch support strip from scrap redwood,

Figure J

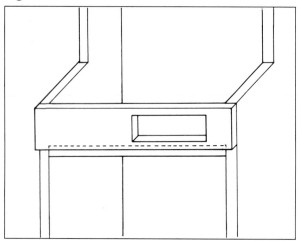

Figure K

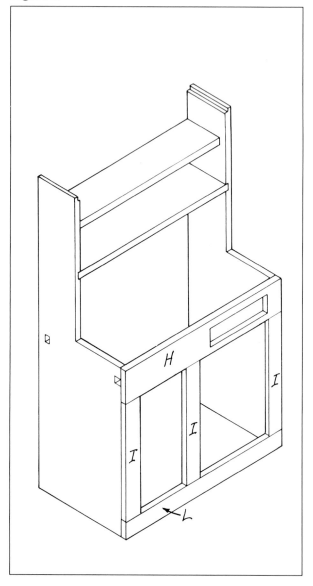

and glue it along the back of the H piece so that it extends ¾ inch below the bottom edge (**Figure J**). Drive a nail through each side wall into the ends of the support brace.

3. Attach the lower horizontal facer (L) to the edges of the walls with all pieces flush at the bottom, and then add the three vertical facers (I) as shown in **Figure K**. The upper end of the center I piece can be glued to both the H piece and the narrow support strip. At the lower end, simply glue it to the L piece. It will be reinforced later. Each outer I piece can be glued and nailed to the support strip at the top, and to the front edge of the cabinet wall along one side.

4. To provide extra support for the counter top, cut two 1½ x 15-inch support strips from scrap redwood or pine. Attach one strip to the inside of each wall, so that the upper edge of the strip is flush with the upper edge of the front portion of the wall. Install the counter top (**G**) and the cabinet top (**A**), and hinge the shelf door (**B**) to the front edge of the cabinet top as shown in **Figure L**.

5. To install the handle, first insert the non-rounded end of one O piece through the mortise that you cut near the front of one wall (**Figure M**). Adjust it so that only about 1 inch extends beyond the wall on the inside, and then glue it to the back of the H piece. Secure the joint with two screws.

6. Cut a 2-inch length of 2 x 4 to use as a glue block for the other handle support. Glue the block to the inside of the wall, along the front edge of the remaining mortise as shown in **Figure N**. Secure it using two screws. Insert the remaining O piece through the mortise and insert the length of closet rod through the holes in the O pieces to insure that they are aligned properly. Attach the rear O piece to the glue block inside the cabinet. Trim the closet rod if it extends beyond the O pieces, and glue it in place.

Figure L   **Figure M**

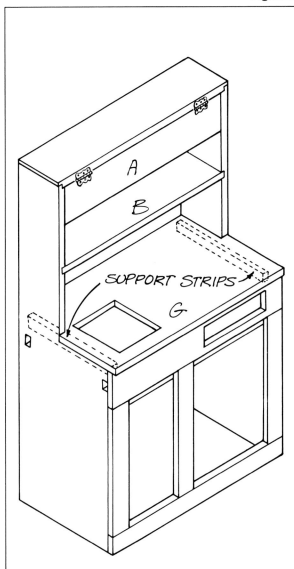

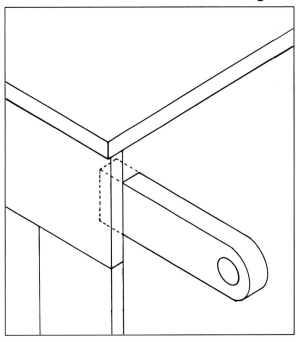

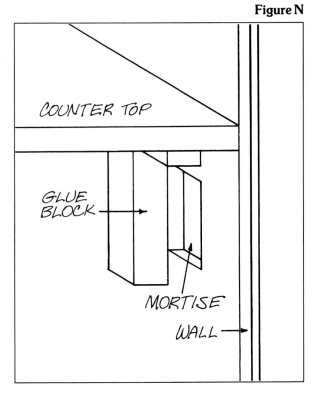

7. The splined **P** piece will serve as the cabinet floor. To give it a little extra strength, cut two 1½ x 15-inch support strips from scrap redwood or pine, and glue and nail them to one side of the floor along the two short edges. Slide the floor into the cabinet from the back so that it butts against the inside surfaces of the walls and lower front facer, with all pieces flush at the bottom. Glue and nail it in place.

Figure O

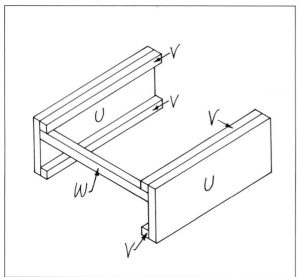

Figure P

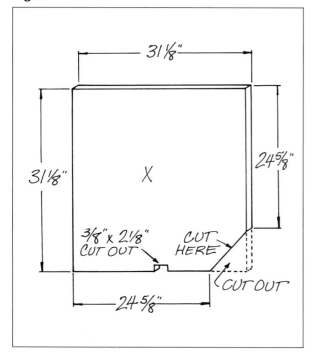

will go toward the front of the cabinet, and the **W** piece at the back will serve as a drawer stop to keep the drawer from being pushed too far into the cabinet. Install the assembly inside the cabinet. The front open end should bracket the ends of the drawer opening, and fit perfectly between the counter top and the narrow strip that runs across the inside of the cabinet front. Secure the drawer guide assembly to the cabinet front and counter top.

9. The waferwood **X** and **Y** pieces will serve as the lower and upper cabinet backs. Glue and nail the **Y** piece to the back edges of the walls and cabinet top, inside the rabbets.

10. Cut the lower right corner from the **X** piece as shown in **Figure P**. In addition, cut a ⅜ x 2⅛-inch rectangle from the center of the lower edge as shown. Save both cutouts.

11. Use the two butt hinges to attach the **X** piece to the lower edge of the **Y** piece. Glue and nail the two cutouts to the back edges of the wall and floor as shown in **Figure Q**, so they fit into their original positions in the **X** piece when it is closed.

12. Install the two parts of the suitcase latch, one near the lower edge of the **X** piece just above the rectangular cutout, and the other on the rectangular cutout itself. Be certain to align them so the latch works properly.

13. Cut two 3-inch lengths of 2 x 4 to serve as axle support blocks, and drill a hole through each block as shown in **Figure R**, using a drill bit that matches the diameter of the metal axle. Glue one block to the bottom of the cabinet, flush with the front corner of the wall that contains the handle. The axle hole should run parallel to the wall, of course. Glue the other block to the bottom of the cabinet, flush with the back corner of the same wall, making sure that the axle holes are aligned. You may wish to insert the axle to be certain they are aligned properly. Secure each block with two 2-inch-long screws inserted up through the block into the cabinet floor. Be sure the screws do not intersect the axle holes.

14. Insert the metal axle through the aligned holes in the blocks, leaving equal extensions on each side. Glue the axle into the blocks. At each end of the axle, install an 8-inch wheel, a washer, and a nut.

8. The drawer guide structure is assembled and then installed inside the cabinet. Use the pine **U**, **V**, and **W** pieces to build the structure, butting them as shown in **Figure O**. The completely open end of the assembly

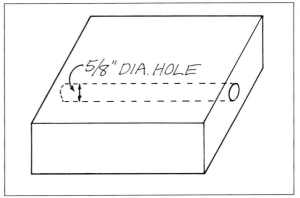

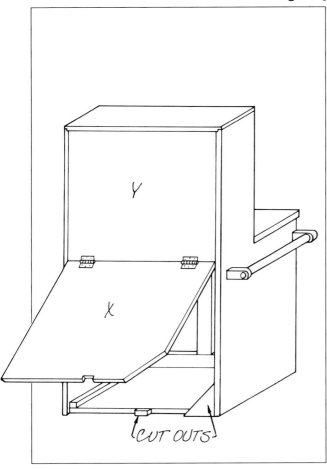

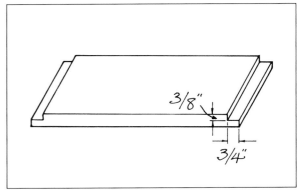

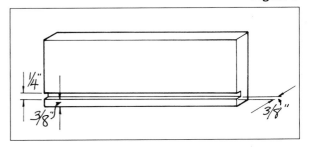

15. Now install the caster wheels at the opposite end of the cabinet. In order to make the cabinet level, we found it necessary to place ½-inch-thick blocks between the caster plates and the cabinet. You may or may not need to use blocks, depending on the height of the caster wheels you purchased. Just place them underneath the cabinet, and cut blocks from scrap wood if necessary before you permanently attach the caster wheels.

Building the Bins and Drawer

1. The **M** pieces will serve as the front and back of the drawer. On one **M** piece, cut a ⅜ x ¾-inch rabbet along the two short edges on one side (**Figure S**). This will be the drawer front.

2. The **N** pieces will serve as the drawer sides. Each **N** piece and each **M** piece must be dadoed to accommodate the waferwood drawer floor. Cut a ¼-inch-wide dado, ⅜ inch deep, along each of these pieces as shown in **Figure T**. Each dado should be cut ⅜ inch from the long lower edge of the piece, on what will be the inside surface. The front **M** piece is the only one that already has inside and outside surfaces designated (by the rabbets you cut in step 1).

Figure U

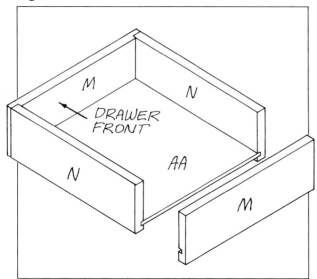

DRAWER FRONT

M N N M AA

Figure V

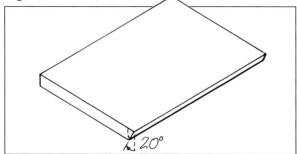

20°

Figure W

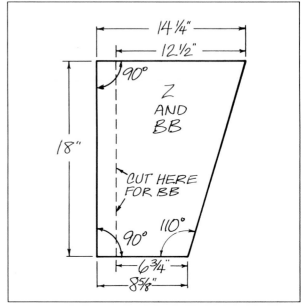

14 ¼"

12 ½"

90°

Z AND BB

18"

CUT HERE FOR BB

90°   110°

6 ¾"

8 ⅝"

3. The waferwood **AA** piece will serve as the drawer floor. Assemble the **M** and **N** pieces around the **AA** piece as shown in **Figure U**. Glue and nail the redwood pieces together at the corners. There's no need to glue the waferwood floor into the dadoes.

4. Attach a drawer pull to the front of the drawer and slide the drawer into the cabinet.

5. The large bin consists of a redwood face (**J**), pine front and back pieces (**Q**), a pine floor (**S**), and waferwood sides (**Z**). The bin assembly is shown in **Figure X**. Begin by beveling one long edge of the **S** piece at a 20-degree angle, as shown in **Figure V**. Bevel one short edge of one **Q** piece, also at a 20-degree angle. This **Q** piece will serve as the bin back.

6. A cutting diagram for the large bin side is provided in **Figure W**. Modify each of the **Z** pieces as shown.

7. Assemble the large bin, butting the pieces as shown in **Figure X**. The front **Q** piece rests on top of the floor (**S**), but the back **Q** piece covers the back beveled edge of the floor. The two sides (**Z**) cover the edges of the front, back, and floor.

8. Round off one short end of the redwood bin face (**J**). Glue it to the front of the bin so that it extends about 3 inches above the front piece and 2 inches below it, placing the rounded end at the bottom. Secure the bin face to the front of the bin with finishing nails driven from inside and attach a drawer pull about 4 inches from the upper edge.

9. Cut a 15-inch length of ¾-inch dowel rod and glue it to the inside of the redwood bin face, butted firmly against the bottom of the floor (**Figure Y**). The dowel should extend equally beyond each side of the bin face. Secure it with a few finishing nails driven through the dowel into the redwood face. Place the bin in the cabinet so that the bin face is flush with the cabinet front and the upper edge of the bin face is as close as possible to the top of the bin opening. There will be a gap between the bottom of the bin face and the bottom of the bin opening, but that's as it should be. On the inside of the cabinet, secure each end of the dowel rod using a conduit clip held in place by two tacks (**Figure Z**).

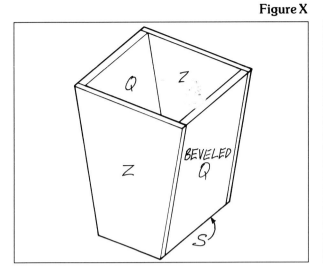

Figure X

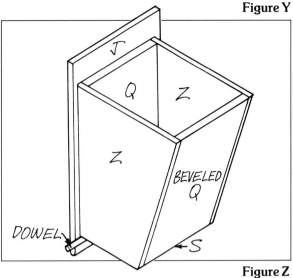

Figure Y

Figure Z

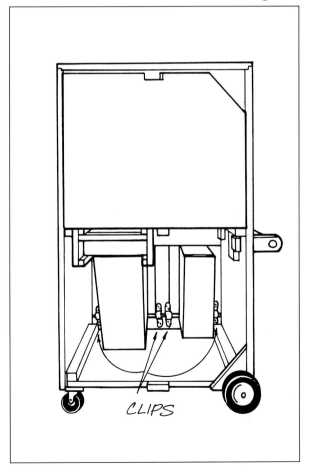

10. The narrower bin is assembled in the same manner, using the pine **R** pieces as the front and back, the waferwood **BB** pieces as the sides, the pine **T** piece as the floor, and the redwood **K** piece as the face. Bevel the back long edge of the floor and the lower short edge of the **R** piece that will serve as the bin back at a 20-degree angle, as you did for the large bin. Follow the cutting diagram provided in **Figure W** to modify the two sides. The front and back **R** pieces will extend up above the waferwood sides when you assemble the bin. The back piece will prevent the bin from falling out of the cabinet when it is opened. Assemble the narrow bin in the same manner as you did the wider one, butting the pieces as shown in **Figure X**. Round off the lower end of the redwood face, and glue it to the bin so that it extends 2 inches above the upper edge of the pine front. Attach a drawer pull.

11. Cut a 12-inch length of dowel rod and use it to fasten the bin in place in the cabinet as you did the wider bin.

Finishing Touches

1. Attach the swiveling plant hanger to the cabinet wall opposite the one with the handle. It will come in handy when you wish to work on a hanging plant.

2. We tacked the leather strap to the same cabinet wall, making loops and tacking the strap to the wall between each loop, to hold gardening tools such as claws, trowels, etc.

PORTABLE POTTING CENTER

Cold Frame

Here's one of the simplest and most practical outdoor structures you'll find —
and the original solar-heating project! True believers tell of growing year-round
veggies using a cold frame to cover a garden dug below the freezing line. The
hinged top slopes so water will run off and features safe plastic panes. Overall
dimensions are 6 x 3 x 1 feet.

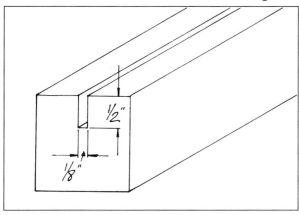

Figure A

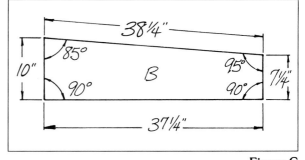

Figure B

Figure C

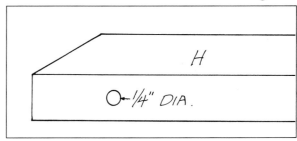

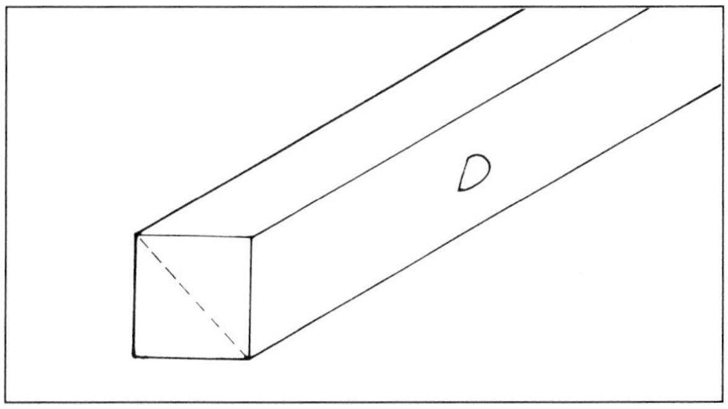

Figure D

Materials

13 linear feet of standard 1 x 12 redwood
34 linear feet of standard 1 x 8 redwood
27 linear feet of standard 2 x 2 redwood
Three pieces of ⅛-inch-thick clear acrylic plastic sheet, each 2 x 3 feet
Two door hinges, each 3 inches long with ¾-inch flanges
1¼-inch No. 6 gauge flathead wood screws
2d galvanized finishing nails
Epoxy glue

Cutting the Wood

1. Cut and label the pieces listed below.

Code	Dimensions in inches	Quantity	Material
Frame Box:			
A	¾ x 7¼ x 74	1	1 x 8
B	¾ x 10¼ x 37¼	2	1 x 12
C	¾ x 11½ x 72½	1	1 x 12
D	1½ x 1½ x 7⅛	2	2 x 2
Frame Lid:			
E	1½ x 1½ x 75½	2	2 x 2
F	1½ x 1½ x 38⅜	2	2 x 2
G	1½ x 1½ x 35	2	2 x 2
H	¾ x 1½ x 23	6	1 x 8
I	¾ x ¾ x 37½	2	1 x 8
J	¾ x ¾ x 69½	1	1 x 8
K	¾ x ¾ x 75½	1	1 x 8

2. Cut a ⅛ x ½-inch groove along what will be the inner side of each **E** and **F** piece, centered between two long edges (**Figure A**). In addition, cut the same size groove along two opposite sides of each **G** piece.

3. A cutting diagram is provided in **Figure B** for the sloping upper edge of the B pieces. Use the dimensions and angles provided to cut the slope on each B piece.

4. Cut each D piece in half along the diagonal, as shown in **Figure C**, to form two glue blocks.

5. Miter both ends of each E and F piece at a 45-degree angle.

6. Drill two ¼-inch-diameter holes through three of the H pieces as shown in **Figure D**.

Figure E

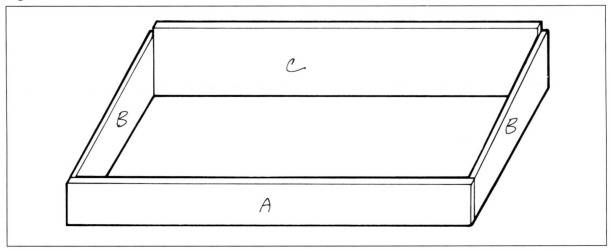

Figure F

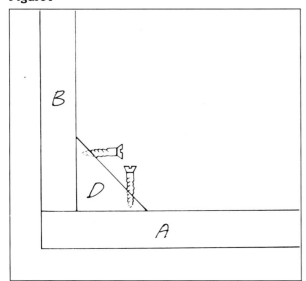

Figure G

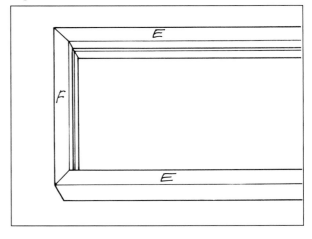

Assembling the Box

1. The assembled box is shown in **Figure E**. Butt the pieces together as shown, with all edges flush at the bottom, and secure the joints with glue and finishing nails. The back (C piece) will extend up beyond the sides.

2. The butt joints are secured in the front and back corners with glue blocks (D pieces), as shown in **Figure F**. Insert screws through each D piece into the box pieces as illustrated.

Assembling the Lid

The assembled lid is shown in **Figure J**. Each pane is installed in the 2 x 2 frame, then the cross supports (H pieces) are installed.

1. The E and F pieces form the basic frame. Attach one E piece to each end of an F piece, using glue and screws, as shown in **Figure G**. Be sure the grooves of all three pieces are even and facing toward the inside of the frame.

2. Slip one pane of plastic into the grooves at the open end of the frame, and slide it all the way down until it engages in the groove in the F piece.

Figure H

Figure I

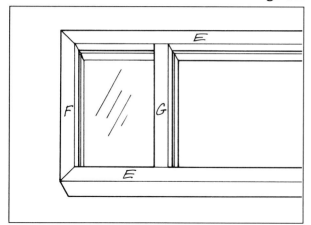

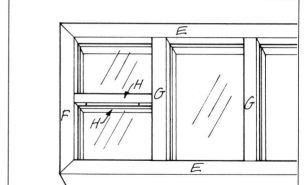

Figure J

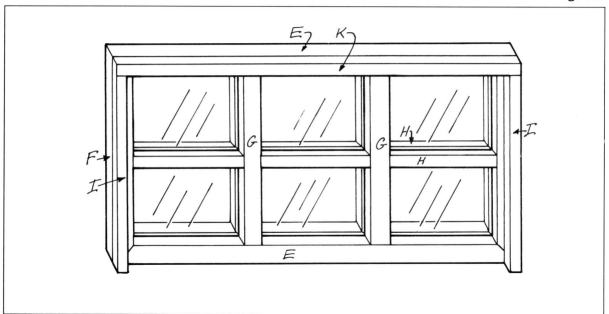

3. Position a **G** piece over the unframed side of the pane, slipping the groove over the edge of the pane (**Figure H**). Secure the **G** piece using glue and a screw inserted through the **E** piece into each end.

4. Repeat this procedure to install two additional plastic panes in the frame. Attach the remaining **F** piece on the opposite end of the frame.

5. Install two **H** pieces (cross supports) aligned one on top and one beneath a pane, as shown in **Figure I**.

Use one of the drilled **H** pieces on top (the holes allow for drainage), and an undrilled piece underneath. Secure the supports by inserting screws up through the lower support and plastic pane into the upper support.

6. Install a pair of **H** pieces on each of the remaining panes in the same manner.

7. Attach the **K** piece along the underside of one **E** piece, even with the front edge as shown in **Figure J**. This will be the front of the framed lid.

COLD FRAME

81

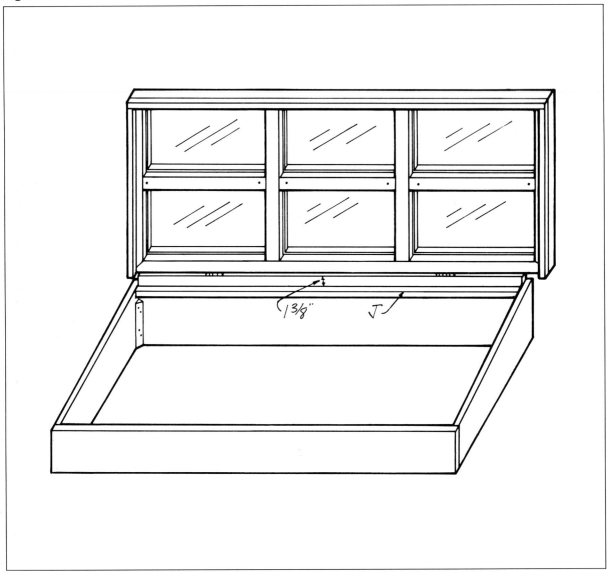

8. Attach one I piece along the underside of one **F** piece, even with the outside edge (**Figure J**), butting the end as shown. Attach the remaining I piece to the opposite F piece in the same manner.

Final Assembly

1. Place the assembled lid over the box section, so the back edge of the lid is snug against the box back.

Install the hinges, positioning each one approximately 1 foot from the end of the cold frame.

2. Attach the J piece 1⅜ inches below the upper edge of the C piece, as shown in **Figure K**. This piece serves as weather stripping.

3. Drill several ¼-inch-diameter drainage holes through the front E piece, but take pains not to damage the panes!

Lawn Care Caddy

If you enjoy working in the yard, this little caddy can be your back's best friend. It's inexpensive, easy to build, and easy to use. Features include a rake rack, storage compartments, shelves, and a trash bag holder. All in a compact 20¾ x 25 x 24½ inches.

Figure A

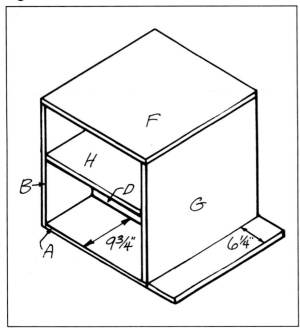

Materials

One 4 x 8 sheet of ⅜-inch exterior-grade plywood

20¾-inch length of 1½-inch-diameter wooden closet rod

40-inch length of ½-inch-diameter wooden dowel rod

15-inch length of standard pine 2 x 4

4-foot length of standard pine 1 x 3

20¾-inch length of ¾ x ¾-inch slat trim

24-inch length of ½-inch-diameter metal rod for the axle. You'll need to drill a ⅛-inch-diameter hole through the rod near each end, to accommodate the cotter pins. If you don't have the tool for this job, you can have the holes drilled at a machine shop.

Two 8-inch-diameter rubber wheels (Old lawn mower wheels will work just fine.)

Two cotter pins

Two spherical wooden drawer pulls, each 1⅜ inches in diameter

Seventy No. 7 gauge flathead wood screws, each 1¼ inches long

A handful of 1 x 18 wire brads, two metal binder clips, exterior glue, and wood sealer or paint

Cutting the Plywood

The pieces listed below are cut from plywood. To avoid confusion later, label each piece as it's cut.

Part	Quantity	Description	Dimension in inches
A	1	Bottom	20 x 24
B	2	Front/Back	20 x 24
C	1	Bin divider	6¼ x 23⅝
D	1	Shelf divider	11 x 17⅜
E	2	Side	7 x 24⅜
F	1	Top	18¼ x 20
G	1	Bin front	20 x 23⅝
H	1	Shelf	17⅜ x 20
J	2	Trim	3 x 20
K	4	Trim	1½ x 24⅜
L	4	Trim	1½ x 17¾
M	2	Bin lid	6⅝ x 10
N	2	Inner lid	6¼ x 9¾

Assembly

We have divided the assembly into several sections. You'll begin by building the front section, then add the back compartments, sides, and trim. The wheels and handle are attached last. To avoid splitting the wood, pre-drill all screw holes, using a bit that is slightly smaller in diameter than the screw shank, and don't use more than three or four screws along any one edge.

Building the Front Section

1. Figure A is an assembly diagram for the front section of the caddy. Begin by attaching the B piece to the A piece, butting the edges as shown. Secure this joint with glue and four screws.

2. Place the D piece along the center of the A piece, as shown, and glue it to the B and A pieces. Place the H piece on top, and glue it to the D and B pieces. Secure both the D and H pieces to the B piece using screws. Also, secure the D piece to the A piece with two screws.

3. Glue the G piece to the A, D, and H pieces. Secure the A-to-G joint with screws, but do not use screws for the other two joints.

4. Attach the F piece using glue and eight screws.

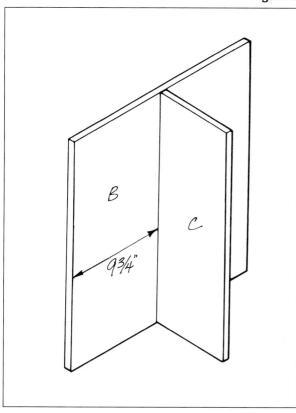

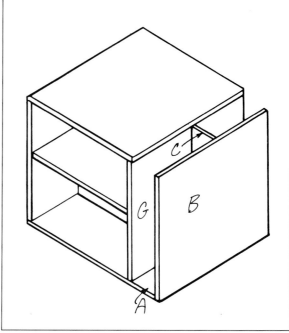

Building the Bin Section

The bin section is shown in **Figure B**. It is assembled separately, then added to the front section.

1. Glue the **C** piece along the center of the **B** piece with the upper ends flush. Secure with two screws.

2. Attach this assembly to the front section as shown in **Figure C**. Secure the B-to-A joint with glue and four screws. Secure the C-to-G joint in the same manner, using only two screws.

3. Attach an **E** piece to each side of the caddy, covering the edges of the G and B pieces (**Figure D**). Secure each E piece with glue and eight screws.

4. Make a lid for each rear compartment by gluing an N piece to the underside of each M piece as shown in **Figure E**. The N piece will be on the bottom of the lid. Drive a screw through the center of each lid, from the bottom up, into a spherical wooden drawer pull.

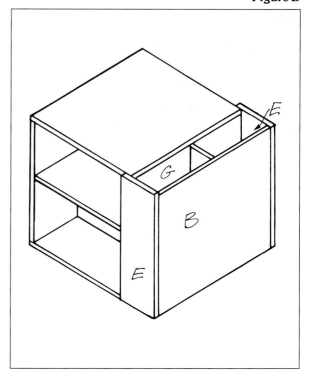

Figure E

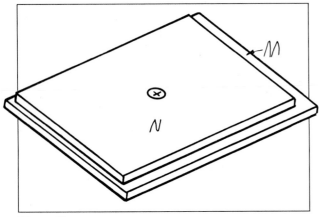

Figure F

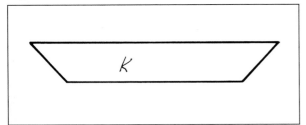

Figure G

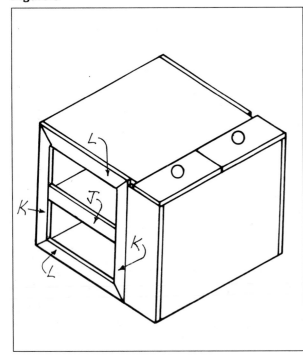

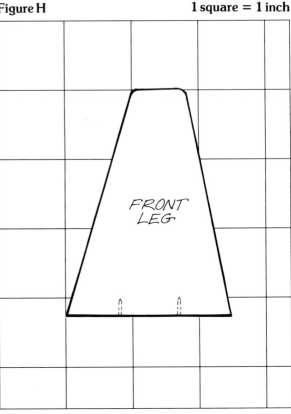

FRONT LEG

Attaching the Trim

1. Miter both ends of each **K** and **L** trim piece at a 45-degree angle (**Figure F**). Use two **K** and two **L** pieces to make a frame on each side of the open section of the caddy (**Figure G**). Use glue and wire brads to attach these pieces.

2. Attach the **J** trim piece to the edge of the **H** piece, using brads, so the shelf has a lip to keep things from falling out as you roll merrily along. (Speaking of rolling, let's see how you're going to get this thing off the ground.)

The Legs and Wheel Assembly

At this point you have built an immovable lawn caddy. Since it's much more useful to be able to roll it about, you'll want to attach wheels and a handle. And don't forget those convenient little front-end doodads, the rake rack, and the trash bag holder.

Figure I Figure J

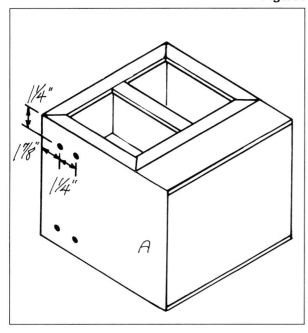

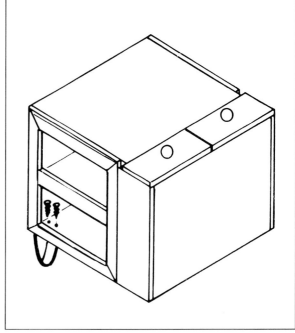

Making the Front Legs

1. Cut two 4½-inch lengths of 2 x 4. You'll want to contour these legs a bit so they'll clear easily when you roll the caddy around. What you basically need is a "V" shape, with slightly more slope on the rear edge of the leg. Enlarge the scale drawing **(Figure H)** and contour each length of 2 x 4.

2. To attach one leg, first drill two starter holes in the underside of the caddy (the **A** piece) as shown in **Figure I**. Drill one hole 1⅞ inches from the front of the caddy, 1¼ inches directly behind the first one. Drill two more holes near the opposite long edge of the A piece, to accommodate the other leg.

3. Drill a starter hole into the top of one leg, 1⅛ inches from the front edge and centered between the sides. Drill another starter hole 1¼ inches directly behind the first one. Drill the remaining leg in the same manner. Glue the legs in place and drive a screw from inside the caddy into each hole **(Figure J)**.

Attaching the Wheels

1. Cut two 3-inch lengths of 2 x 4 to use as axle mounts. Drill a ½-inch-diameter hole for the axle rod

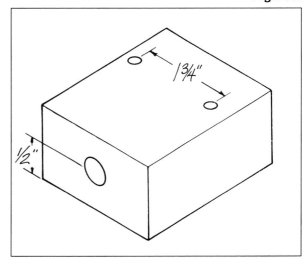

through the length of each mount, centered ½ inch from the upper surface **(Figure K)**. Drill two starter holes through each mount, 1¾ inches apart, on either side of the axle hole. Enlarge each starter hole slightly, on the bottom of the mount, so you can countersink the screws. Attach each mount to the underside of the

Figure L

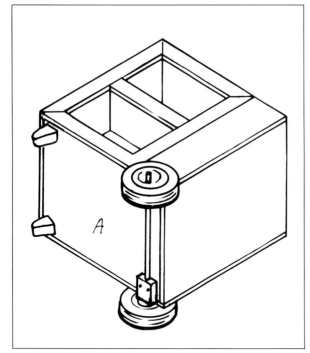

A

Figure M   1 square = 1 inch

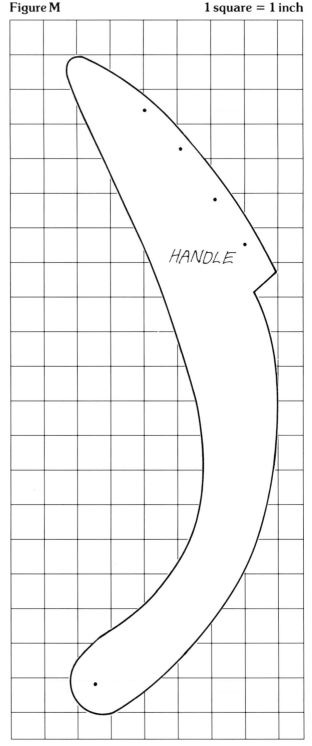

HANDLE

caddy, 3¼ inches from the back and flush with the out-side edge (**Figure L**). The screws will protrude through the bottom of the caddy into the compartments, where they won't interfere with its operation or safety. If you like, cover the screw points with small wood blocks.

Assembling the Handle

1. Enlarge the scale drawing of the handle (**Figure M**) and cut two handle pieces from plywood. Drill a starter hole at each point indicated on the drawing, and enlarge the holes on the opposite sides of the two pieces so you can countersink the screws.

2. Attach one handle piece to the left side of the caddy (**Figure N**). The small notch in the handle above the screw holes mounts flush with the top of the **E** piece at the upper back corner of the caddy. Attach the re-maining handle piece to the opposite side of the caddy. The protruding points of these screws should be shaved off, since they might injure someone using the rear compartments of the caddy.

3. Sandwich the length of closet rod between the two handle pieces, using one screw in each end.

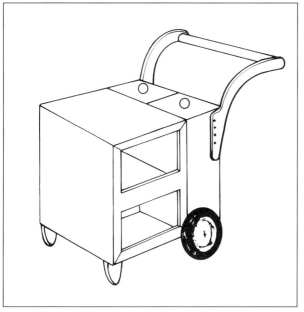

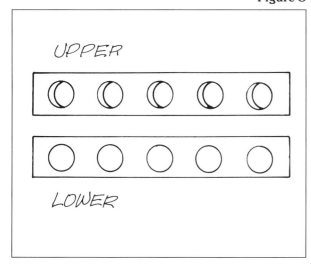

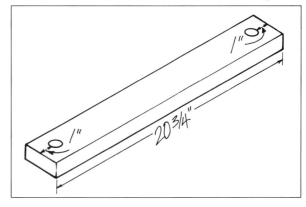

Building the Rake Rack

1. Cut the 1 x 3 into two 20¾-inch lengths. Drill five evenly-spaced 1½-inch-diameter holes through one of these pieces (**Figure O**). This will be the top rack. Drill five 1½-inch-diameter shallow sockets into the remaining piece, matching the placement of the holes in the top rack.

2. Drill four screw holes into the front of the caddy (B piece), 1 inch from the top (**Figure P**). Drill four more screw holes 1¼ inches from the bottom of the caddy front. Attach the racks by driving screws through the B piece into each rack.

Adding the Trash Bag Holder

1. Cut the ½-inch dowel rod into two 20-inch lengths. Drill a ½-inch-diameter shallow socket into one surface of the slat trim, 1 inch from each end, as shown in **Figure Q**.

Figure R

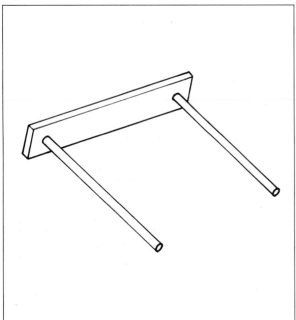

Figure T

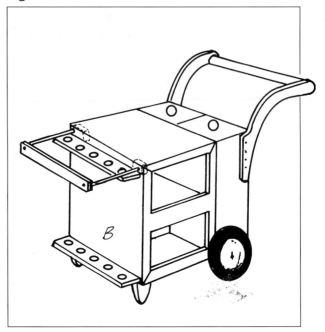

Figure S

2. Insert one length of the dowel rod into each socket and drive a brad from the opposite side to secure it (**Figure R**). This is the basic holder.

3. The holder slides in and out of the caddy front. Drill a 9/16-inch-diameter hole through the front (B piece) of the caddy, just above the upper rack and 1 inch from the side (**Figure S**). Drill an identical hole near the opposite side, as shown.

4. The ends of the holder are steadied by guide blocks inside the caddy (**Figure T**). Cut two 3-inch lengths of 1 x 3. Drill a 9/16-inch-diameter hole through the length of each piece, 3/8 inch from the surface.

5. Slip the trash bag holder into the holes in the front of the caddy. Slide one guide block onto each dowel rod and glue one block inside each front corner of the caddy (**Figure T**). Drive a nail into the end of each dowel rod, and bend it so the trash bag holder won't slide out of the guide blocks. Use a binder clip on each side to hold a garbage bag in place.

Finishing

Stain the caddy if you like. It should be sealed with clear wood sealer, or painted to make it weatherproof.

Hot Tub

After a hard day at the salt mines what could be more relaxing than a nice long soak in a hot tub of bubbling water? Well all right, so maybe it's the second most relaxing thing, but it's pretty darned close! The "hot tub experience" is sweeping the country, and for good reason – you just can't get more enjoyment for your investment. Rest your weary bones in this 6-foot-diameter redwood hot tub and let the rest of the world just float on by.

Figure A

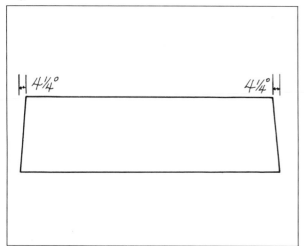

Figure B

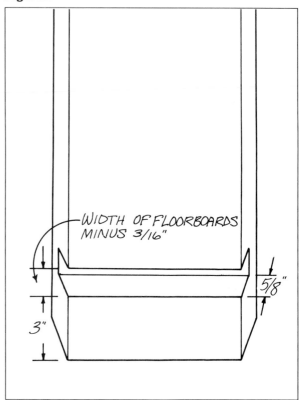

Materials

Because a hot tub must be strong and yet absorb water in order to swell and seal the gaps between boards, the selection of wood is very important. Redwood, the traditional material for hot tubs, is the best. When purchasing redwood, look for boards that are straight, vertically grained (all heart), clear of all knots, and kiln dried. BE PICKY!! Check each board and don't take second best even if it means buying from several lumberyards.

180 linear feet of 2 x 6 redwood
56 linear feet of 2 x 12 redwood
24 linear feet of 4 x 4 redwood
12 linear feet of 2 x 8 redwood
Four lengths of ⅜-inch flexible steel, each 20-feet-long and threaded at both ends.
Four ⅜-inch lugs
Hot tub plumbing kit (see Plumbing)

Cutting the Wood

Cut the pieces listed below from redwood.

Part	Material	Length	Quantity
Staves	2 x 6	4 feet	45
Floorboards	2 x 12	8 feet	7
Chine Joists	4 x 4	6 feet	4
Seats	2 x 8	6 feet	2

The Staves

The staves make up the wall of the hot tub. Each stave's edges are beveled so that when put together edge to edge they will form a 6-foot-diameter circle (**Figure A**). On the inside (narrow side) of each stave and 3 inches from its bottom edge, a groove is cut to accept the floor of the tub (**Figure B**).

1. Cut each stave EXACTLY 4 feet in length. Use a square to mark the cut and to insure that the top of the stave is flat.

2. Set your table saw blade at a 4¼-degree angle. To get the ¼ degree, you may have to use a protractor. Make every effort to achieve this exact angle (4¼ degrees = 4 degrees 15 minutes). Bevel each stave EXCEPT ONE, as shown if **Figure A**. If you do not have a table saw, most lumber yards will perform this task for a fee. Make sure they know the importance of getting a precise angle.

Figure C

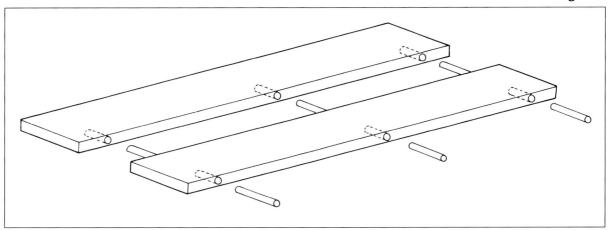

3. Measure the thickness of the floorboard material. The groove on the inside of each stave must be ³/₁₆ inch NARROWER than the flooring material to insure a tight fit when the staves are pounded onto the floorboards. Measure 3 inches from the bottom of each stave and use a square to mark what will be the lower edge of the groove. Use a router or a dado saw to cut the appropriate width groove ⅝ inch deep into each stave. Groove the last unbeveled stave as well.

4. Find a dry place to store the staves so that they do not absorb moisture and swell while you build the floor of the tub.

The Floorboards

The floor of the hot tub is a 6-foot-diameter circle made from 2 x 12s doweled together side by side.

1. Use a doweling gig to drill three ³/₈-inch-diameter sockets, 1 inch deep, into the edges of the floorboards to be joined. Drill one hole at the center of the board edges, and drill two additional holes 18 inches from either end. Join the boards using 2-inch lengths of ³/₈-inch dowel (**Figure C**). You can use mastic tape, but only on the lower half (the bottom side of the floor) of the joints. If the mastic seeps into the tub area it will cause a slick spot in the floor of your tub.

2. To draw the 6-foot-diameter circle that will become the tub floor, use a piece of lath with a hole drilled in one end to fit a pencil point. Drive a small nail through the lath exactly 3 feet from the tip of the pencil.

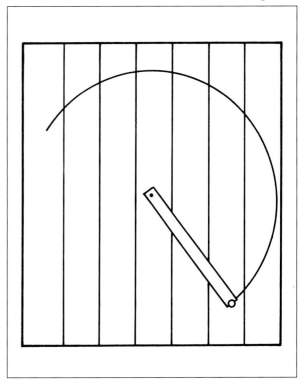

Select a spot at the center of the assembled floorboards and press in the nail. Rotate the lath to draw a 6-foot-diameter circle with the pencil (**Figure D**). Measure the diameter several different ways; the circle must be as perfect as possible.

Figure E

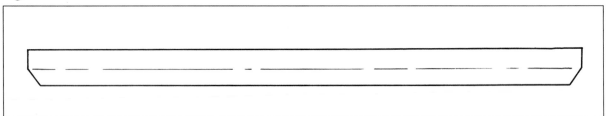

Figure F

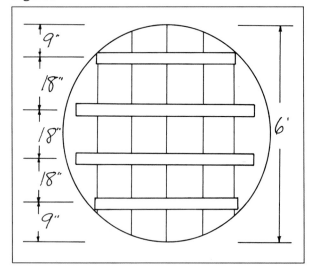

Figure G

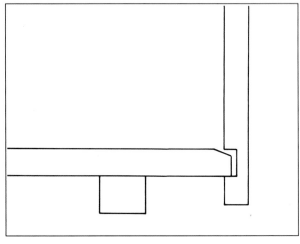

3. A saber saw is the best tool for cutting the circle. Take your time and stay just to the outside edge of the pencil line.

4. Attach several lengths of lath across the floorboards to make sure everything stays in place when moving the floor.

5. Pick the best side to be the inside of the tub floor. Chamfer the edge of this side slightly (**Figure E**) so that the floorboards will fit more easily into the grooves cut in the staves.

6. Turn the floorboard assembly over to attach the 4 x 4 chine joists.

7. The chine joists will be placed perpendicular to the floorboards and 18 inches apart (**Figure F**). Place the chine joists in position and mark either end at least 3 inches in from the edges of the floor. Cut the chine joists and toenail them to the floorboards with 6d common nails, making sure that the nails do not go through the tub side of the floor.

8. The assembled floor can now be turned over and placed at the final position of the hot tub.

9. Drill a 2⁵⁄₁₆-inch-diameter hole through the floor, 6 inches from one edge, for the drain. Install the drain through the floor. Use Teflon and PVC weld on all threaded fittings to give a watertight seal. Attach a short length of PVC pipe, a PVC elbow, and a hose bib extending past the edge of the floor (see the section on plumbing the hot tub). This portion of the plumbing is installed now so you won't have to tip the hot tub on its side after the staves are attached.

Staving

"Staving" is the act of assembling the staves and floor in a barrel fashion.

1. Select a point where two floorboards meet, and use your hand to lightly tap a stave into position so that the floorboard joint is at the center of the stave. Use a rubber hammer to tap the stave halfway onto the floor but no farther (**Figure G**).

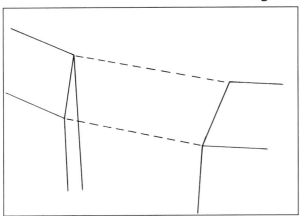

2. Position a second stave against the first and tap this stave into position halfway onto the floor. Give the edge of the stave a sharp blow to force it against the first stave. Repeat this step with a third stave.

3. With three staves in place, return to the first stave and pound it fully onto the floor assembly.

4. Mount a fourth stave as in Step 2, and then return to the second stave and pound it fully into position. Use small pieces of duct tape to hold the tops of the staves together as you pound each stave fully into position. Continue this procedure around the floor until the last unbeveled stave and one empty space around the floor is left.

5. Measure the remaining space at the bottom of the tub. The remaining stave may need to be ripped lengthwise to this width.

6. You may need to bevel for this stave differently than the others. Measure the width of the space at the bottom of the tub, both inside and out. Use these measurements to make a full scale drawing of the end view of this stave (see **Figure H**).

7. Measure the angles with a protractor and set the table saw to make the bevel cuts for the final stave.

8. Position the stave and pound into place.

Hoops

The wall of the hot tub is held in place by four steel hoops. There is a tremendous amount of outward pressure caused by the 1,000 gallons of water necessary to fill this hot tub. Position and tighten the hoops carefully.

If they're too loose and the hot tub will leak excessively; too tight and the staves could be damaged.

1. Measure from the bottom of the tub and mark the following heights in several places around the hot tub: 4 inches; 14 inches; 28 inches and 44 inches. These will be the positions of the hoops.

2. Drive several nails into the staves around the hot tub at the 4-inch level. The first hoop will rest on these nails until it can be tightened.

3. Repeat Step 2 for each of the remaining marked heights, staggering the lugs so that no two are against the same stave (see **Figure I**).

Figure I

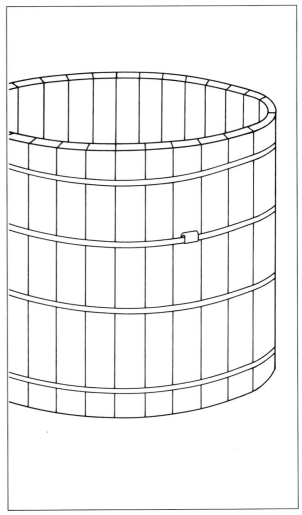

Figure J

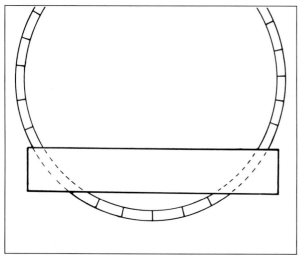

4. First, tighten the bottom hoop moderately until it will stay firmly in place without the nails, then move to the next hoop up, repeating the tightening process for all four hoops. Pound the staves with the rubber mallet from the inside of the tub to keep them in position as you tighten the hoops. Tighten each hoop gradually and in order until all four show 70 pounds of torque on a torque wrench. Care should be taken not to over-tighten the hoops, as it will chip the edges of the staves.

5. Pound on the hoops with the rubber mallet and again check the tightness with the torque wrench, tight-ening if necessary.

6. Sand the tops and corners of the staves to remove any sharp edges.

Benches

Getting the benches inside the hot tub to the best height takes a little imagination and testing. The water level should come up just below the occupant's neck and shoulders. The thing to remember is: Not all occu-pants are the same height. What's comfy for a six-footer may wash the shorter folks away! Climb into the tub, imagine where the water level will be, and crouch down in a sitting position. When everthing looks right, mark that seat position. It may be wise to do the same with family members, or just install several seats at different levels for odd-size friends who may drop by for a dip. Round all seat edges for comfort.

1. Place a 2 x 8 across the top of the hot tub. The distance you place this from the side is entirely up to you. If only two seats are to be installed, it makes little difference, but if seats are to be positioned all around they will need to be closer to the sides to save leg room.

2. From inside the tub, mark a line on the 2 x 8 where it overlaps the tub walls (**Figure J**).

3. Cut along these lines. Cut two 2-inch-wide seat braces from either end of the scrap pieces, following the same curved lines used for the seats.

4. Position and attach the seat braces to the tub wall using 3-inch screws. When attaching the seat braces, make sure the screws go into the center of a stave and not between staves.

5. Attach the seat to the seat braces using 2-inch screws, countersunk to insure that no rough metal edges are exposed.

Plumbing

The best idea for plumbing the hot tub is to buy a kit from a local spa and pool equipment dealer. This will include everything needed to finish the hot tub: a pump, filter, heater, hydrojets, and all pipes and hoses. By buying everything together, you have the confi-dence of knowing that everything will fit and work to-gether. The dealer will need to know how big the hot tub is: 1,000 gallons.

You will still need to drill holes in the hot tub for water inlet and outlet and hydrojets, but it is best to wait until you have the parts (and instructions) in hand to drill the right size holes.

Once you have the plumbing installed...

Fill It Up

Fill the hot tub using a garden hose (it will take a while). It will also take several days for the hot tub to absorb enough water to swell and stop all the leaks — a new hot tub will leak like a sieve, so don't panic! If after several days there are still a few leaks, contact a carpenter or hot tub dealer and inquire about water-proof substances to fill leaking gaps.

Now turn on the pump, then the heater, and give it a couple of hours to heat up. Then climb in and grin — it's standard equipment!

The Visual Hot Tub Sensation

You will find that a hot tub will become a focal point of family leisure and conversation. As great as the sensation is inside a hot tub, the visual setting should be just as relaxing.

The illustrations shown here are examples of what can be done to make your hot tub experience a totally enjoyable one. While the basic hot tub remains the same, an entirely different environment can be created around it with just a little imagination.

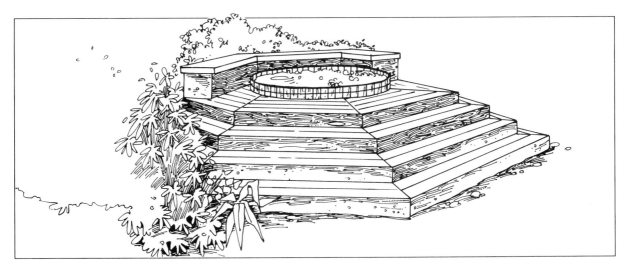

Freestanding Tree House

You say there's no tree in your back yard? Not to worry – this tree house doesn't need one! And instead of just leaves and bark, it has a slide, ladder, swing, jungle gym, and sandbox. Overall dimensions of the basic house are 7 x 7 x 12 feet; the swing beam extends about 16 feet from one end, and the slide extends about 9 feet from one side.

Materials

60 linear feet of rough cedar 4 x 6
50 linear feet of rough cedar 4 x 4
4 linear feet of rough cedar 2 x 12
55 linear feet of rough cedar 2 x 8
30 linear feet of rough cedar 2 x 6
30 linear feet of rough cedar 1 x 6
80 linear feet of rough cedar 1 x 4
45 linear feet of rough cedar 1 x 2
30 linear feet of pine 2 x 6
130 linear feet of pine 2 x 4
40 linear feet of pine 1 x 12
15 linear feet of 1½-inch-diameter wooden closet rod
Two 4 x 8-foot sheets of ¾-inch waferwood or exterior
plywood
Seven 4 x 8-foot sheets of ½-inch waferwood or exterior plywood
One 4 x 8-foot sheet of ⅛-inch masonite
11 linear feet of steel roof flashing, at least 16 inches
wide, to cover the slide
Tarpaper and shingles
3d and 8d galvanized nails
Four bags of cement
Approximately 40 feet of rope or nylon cord, and an
old tire or swing seat (preferably the soft, belt type)
Eight L-brackets
Eight bolts, each 4 inches long, with washers and nuts
for footings
Eight lag screws, each 6 inches long and at least ¼-inch
in diameter

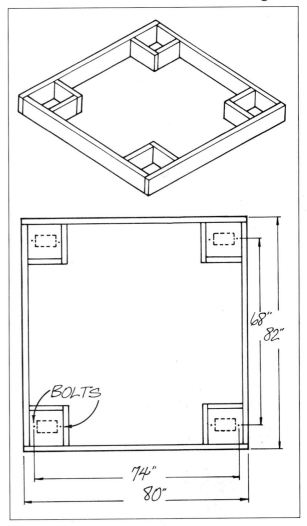

Selecting a Site

The tree house is a good bit higher and longer than the average swing set or climbing bars. To help you visualize where in your yard to put the tree house, consider these points: Is there enough ground space to accommodate children playing on the slide, swing, and jungle gym? We recommend a minimum of 20 x 30 feet. Is there enough overhead space to accommodate the 12-foot-high roof and swing beam without running into overhead wires or tree limbs? Also, consider varying our design (see pages 112-113).

Building the Footings

1. Mark out an 80 x 82-inch rectangle with stakes and string at the site you've selected. Once you're satisfied that you have the tree house positioned where you want it, and the corners are square and true, you're ready to pour the footings.

2. Our four concrete footings (one at each corner) are each 12 inches square, and approximately 3½ inches thick. To insure that all four footings are level, we built a 2 x 4 form around the outside perimeter of the site (**Figure A**). Level the form by adjusting the soil

Figure B

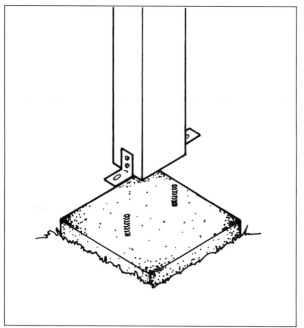

Figure C

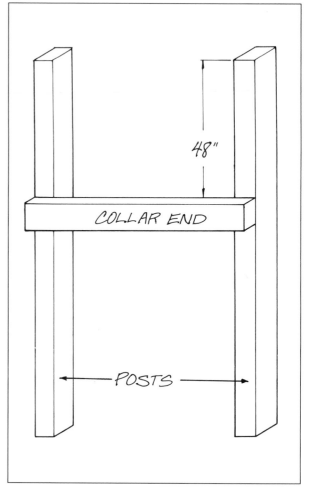

under it, then use scrap boards to close any gaps between the corners and the ground. Mix the concrete according to the manufacturer's directions (see the Tips & Techniques section). With the form in place and level, simply fill each footing form to the top to insure a uniform height.

3. While the concrete is still wet, set two threaded bolts upright into each footing (**Figure B**), so that L-brackets attached to the posts will fit down over the bolts. The L-brackets are attached on either side of the 4 x 6 cedar posts so that the posts can then be fastened securely atop the footings using washers and nuts. Cedar, for all its strength and beauty, eventually will rot when set into concrete, and this method makes it easier to stand the posts.

Standing the Posts

The posts support the entire structure, so take your time and make sure they're aligned and the corners square. If your building site isn't level, your posts will have to be varied in length to compensate for the drop or rise. The tops of the posts must all be at the same height, or the treehouse will not be structurally sound.

1. Cut the pieces listed here from cedar. Note: Unlike planed lumber, the dimensions of the rough cedar we used measure only approximately ¼ (not the usual ½) inch less than the stated size. Check the rough lumber you purchased and make any adjustments to these measurements before you cut any pieces.

Description	Length	Quantity	Size
Post	10 feet	4	4 x 6
Sandbox Side	8 feet	2	2 x 8
Sandbox End	6 feet	2	2 x 8
Collar Side	83½ inches	2	2 x 6
Collar End	72 inches	2	2 x 6

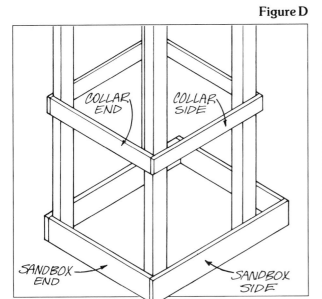

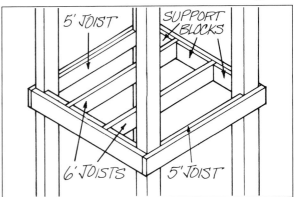

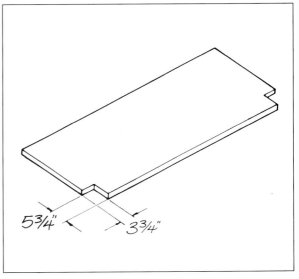

2. Stand the posts in pairs by nailing them to the collar pieces, then joining the pairs using the remaining collar pieces. Place two Posts on the ground approximately 6 feet apart, and nail one Collar End piece between them, 48 inches from what will be the upper ends (**Figure C**). Repeat this procedure using the remaining Posts and Collar End piece.

3. Stand one pair of posts on their footings, and brace the assembly temporarily using a scrap board. Stand the remaining post assembly in the same manner.

4. Nail one Collar Side piece between the two post assemblies on each side, making sure they are even with the Collar End pieces.

5. Attach each Post to its footing using L-brackets and nuts.

6. Nail the Sandbox Sides and Ends to the Posts as shown in **Figure D**. Be sure the sandbox extends beyond the Posts on the opposite end of the site from where you plan to place the swing assembly.

Building the Floor

1. From pine 2 x 6, cut two Joists, each 6 feet long. Nail the Joists between the Collar End pieces as shown in **Figure E**. Cut two additional joists from 2 x 6, each 5 feet long. Nail them to the Collar Side pieces as

shown in **Figure E**. The upper edges of the Joists and collar pieces should be even. Cut three support blocks to fit between the Joists along each Collar End piece. Nail the support blocks to the Collar End pieces as shown in **Figure E**.

2. Cut two Floor pieces from ¾-inch waferwood or exterior plywood: one 48 x 75½; one 27 x 75½ inches. A cutting diagram is provided in **Figure F** for the cutout around the Posts at each corner. Cut two corners out of each Floor piece.

3. Place the larger Floor piece across the Joists and nail. Place the smaller piece across the Joists, butting the edge against the larger piece, and nail.

Figure G

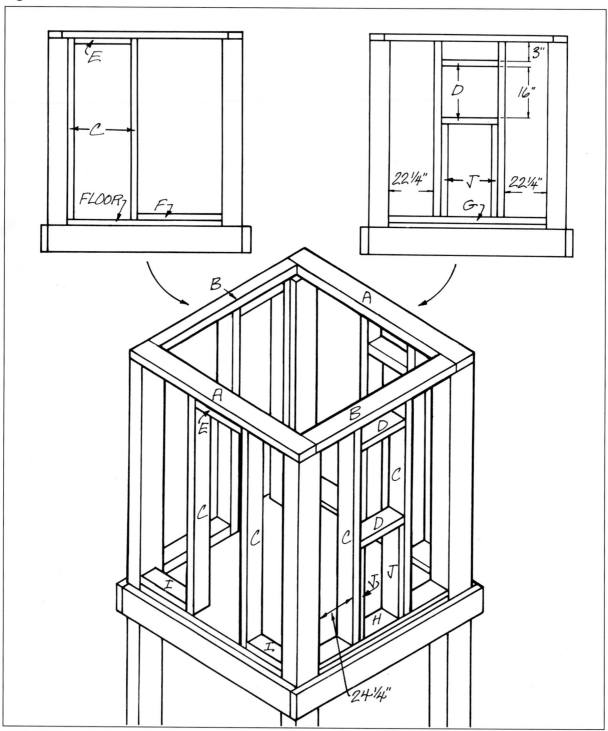

Figure H

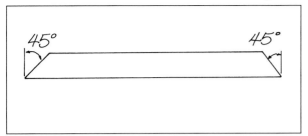

Figure I

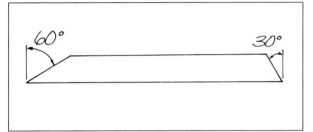

Figure J

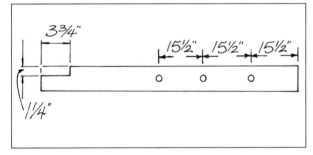

Framing the Walls

1. Cut the pieces listed here from 2 x 4.

Code	Length	Quantity
A	72 inches	2
B	65 inches	2
C	46½ inches	8
D	13 inches	4
E	24 inches	2
F	35 inches	1
G	64½ inches	1
H	60½ inches	1
I	20½ inches	2
J	24½ inches	4

2. The assembled wall frames are shown in **Figure G**. Two walls have framed openings for doorways; the remaining walls have framed openings for windows. To begin, nail the plate (**A** and **B** pieces) to the upper ends of the Posts, butting the ends as shown. Nail the F, G, H, and I pieces on top of the floor piece, butting the ends against the Posts as shown. On each wall, nail two studs (**C** pieces) between the plate and floor pieces, using two D pieces between the studs on the window walls, and an E piece between the studs on the doorway walls. Nail one J piece below the D piece on each side of the window frames, as shown. Wait to frame the roof until you've built the swing assembly below.

Building the Swing Assembly

1. Cut the pieces listed here from rough cedar.

Code	Length	Quantity	Size
A	7 feet	4	4 x 4
B	8 feet	2	4 x 4
C	59½ inches	4	2 x 6
D	20 inches	11	dowel
E	63¼ inches	2	2 x 6
F	47¾ inches	1	4 x 4
G	23½ inches	2	2 x 8
H	16 feet	1	4 x 6

2. Miter both ends of each C and each E piece at a 45-degree angle, as shown in **Figure H**.

3. Miter one end of the F piece at a 30-degree angle, and the other end at a 60-degree angle, as shown in **Figure I**.

4. Cut a 1¼ x 3¾-inch rabbet in one end of each A piece, as shown in **Figure J**. This will be the upper end. In addition, drill a 1½-inch-diameter socket, 2 inches deep, 15½ inches from the opposite end of each A piece. Drill two additional sockets of the same size, spacing them at 15½-inch intervals above the first one. Drill the sockets in what will be the inner sides of each A piece when they are assembled as ladders as shown in **Figure K**.

5. Drill five sockets, each 1½ inches in diameter and 2 inches deep into each B piece, spacing them at 15½-inch intervals along the same side.

Figure K

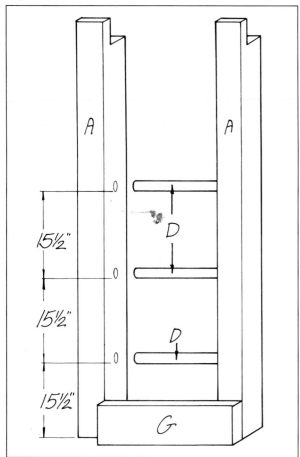

Figure L

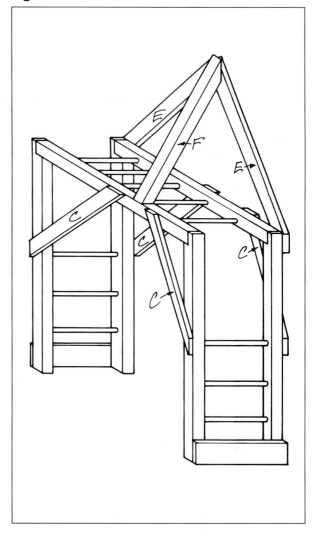

6. One assembled ladder is shown in **Figure K**. The A pieces serve as rails, and the D pieces serve as the rungs. To begin, glue a rung D into each socket of one A piece. Slip the rung ends into the sockets of the opposite A piece. Nail the G piece to the A pieces at the lower end of the ladder, as shown. Build an additional ladder in the same manner.

7. The upper ladder section is assembled in the same manner as the ladders you just constructed. Assemble the upper ladder using the two B pieces as the rails and the remaining D pieces as rungs.

8. Assemble the three ladder sections as shown in **Figure L**, placing the ends of the horizontal ladder into the rabbets in the vertical ladders. Nail the four braces (C pieces) in place as shown.

9. Assemble the swing beam support as shown in **Figure L**, using the E and F pieces. Attach the beam support on top of the ladder assembly (**Figure L**).

10. You're going to need a few helpers to lift the beam for the swing (H piece) into place atop the tree house, so call in the troops. Place the ladder assembly approximately 16 feet from the end of the tree house with the center doorway opening. Center the beam over the doorway, and toe-nail it in place (**Figure M**). Make sure the beam is level, then toe-nail it to the beam support on the ladder assembly (**Figure N**).

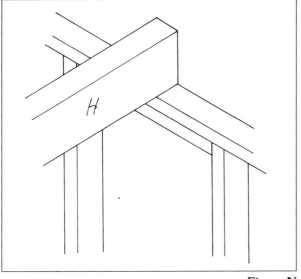

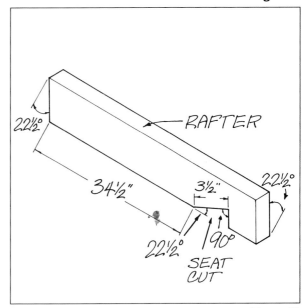

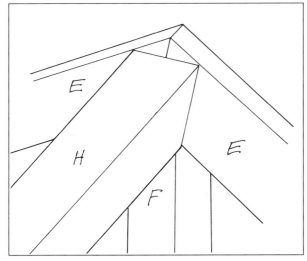

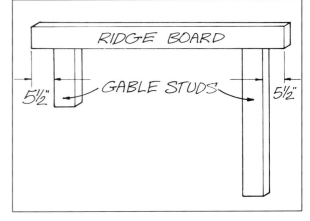

Framing the Roof

1. Cut the pieces listed here from 2 x 4.

Description	Length	Quantity
Rafter	45¾ inches	8
Gable Stud	7½ inches	1
Gable Stud	13½ inches	1
Ridge Board	82 inches	1

2. Miter both ends of each Rafter at a 22½-degree angle, as shown in **Figure O**. Make a seat cut near one end of each Rafter (**Figure O**).

3. The roof frame consists of a ridge assembly (Gable Studs and Ridge Board), which is assembled first, and to which the Rafters are nailed. The ridge assembly is shown in **Figure P**. To build it, nail one Gable Stud 5½ inches from one end of the Ridge Board, as shown. Nail the remaining Gable Stud 5½ inches from the opposite end of the Ridge Board.

Figure Q

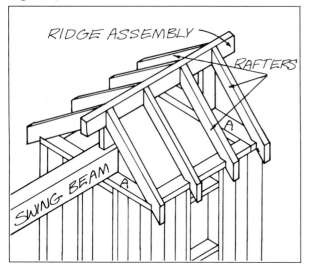

4. The assembled roof frame is shown in **Figure Q**. To begin, mark the center of the plate (**A** piece) on each end of the tree house frame. Nail the ridge assembly to the plate on one end, and to the swing beam on the opposite end, as shown. Nail the rafters to the ridge assembly and plate, placing the seat cut over the plate, as shown.

Sheeting the Walls, Soffit, and Roof

1. Cut the pieces listed here from ½-inch waferwood or exterior plywood.

Code	Dimensions	Quantity
A	18½ x 72 inches	2
B	6¾ x 77 inches	2
C	5 x 44 inches	4
D	24½ x 48 inches	2
E	42¼ x 48 inches	1
F	7¼ x 48 inches	1
G	73 x 48 inches	1
H	72 x 48 inches	1
I	44 x 82 inches	2

2. A cutting diagram for the **A** pieces (gables) is provided in **Figure R**. Cut each gable according to the diagram, but cut the large notch for the swing beam in one gable only.

Figure R

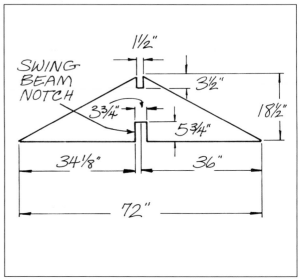

Figure S

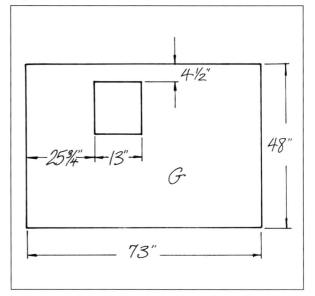

3. A cutting diagram for the window opening in the **G** piece is provided in **Figure S**. A cutting diagram for the window opening in the **H** piece is provided in **Figure T**. Cut the window openings as indicated.

4. Nail the walls (**D**, **E**, **F**, **G**, and **H** pieces) to the frame, butting the edges as shown in **Figure U**. Each fits between the collar and the rafters, as illustrated.

Figure V

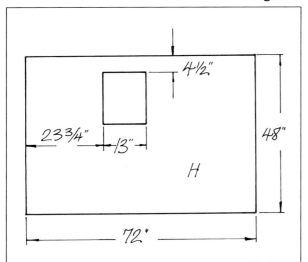

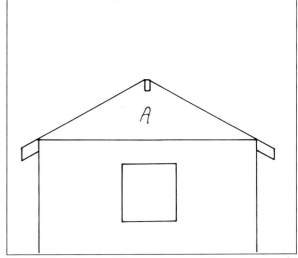

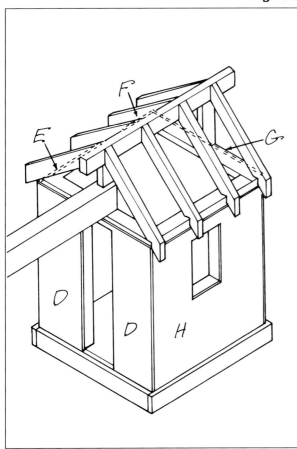

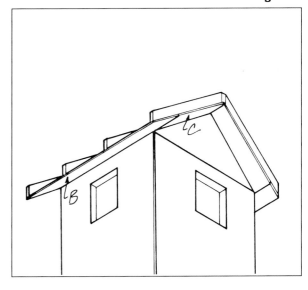

5. Nail one gable (**A** piece) on each end of the frame, butting the lower edge against the wall pieces as shown in **Figure V**.

6. Nail the side soffits **B** to the undersides of the rafters, as shown in **Figure W**. Nail the remaining soffits **C** to the undersides of the rafters, butting the ends at the peak as shown in **Figure W**.

7. Nail each roof piece **I** to the rafters, butting the edges at the peak.

Figure X

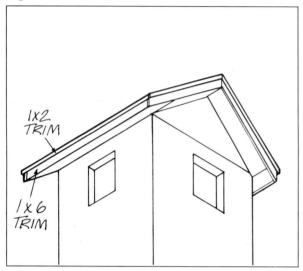

Figure Y

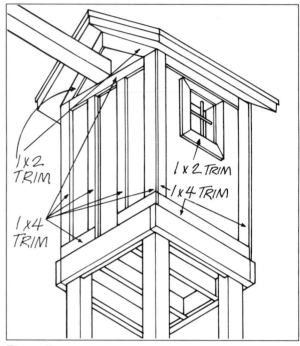

Figure Z

Adding the Trim and Shingles

1. Cut six trim pieces to fit around the roof from rough cedar 1 x 6. Install the trim by attaching it to the rafters as shown in **Figure X**.

2. Cut six trim pieces to create an additional layer of trim around the roof from rough cedar 1 x 2. Install this trim over the wider trim you installed in step 1.

3. Spread the tarpaper over the roof, and attach the shingles, starting at the lower edge and working to the peak (see the Tips & Techniques section for pointers on installing shingles).

4. Cut additional trim pieces from 1 x 2 and 1 x 4 and install them as shown in **Figure Y**.

Building the Slide and Stairs

1. Cut the pieces listed here from rough cedar 2 x 6.

Description	Length	Quantity
Side	82 inches	2
Step	24 inches	8

2. Miter both ends of each Side piece at a 30-degree angle, as shown in **Figure Z**. In addition, miter one end of each Side piece at a 60-degree angle (**Figure Z**).

3. Mount the Steps between the Sides at a 30-degree angle, spacing them 7½ inches apart (**Figure AA**).

4. Install the stair assembly so that it leads up to the doorway opening, and secure it by inserting two lag screws through the collar into each Side.

5. Cut the pieces listed here.

Description	Length	Quantity	Material
Lip	10 feet	2	pine 1 x 12
Trim	10 feet	2	pine 1 x 12
Support	114½ inches	2	cedar 2 x 8
Foot	2 feet	2	cedar 2 x 12
Brace	12¼ inches	2	cedar 2 x 8

6. So that the slide will have a gentle curve at the top and bottom, the Lip, Trim, Support, and Foot pieces

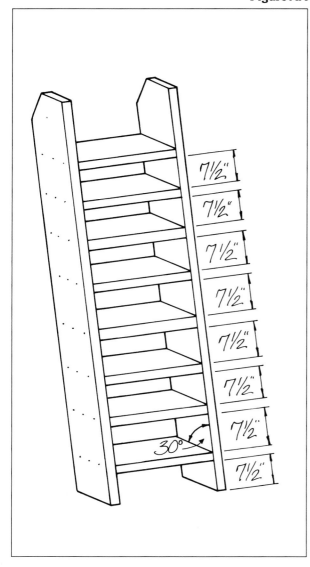

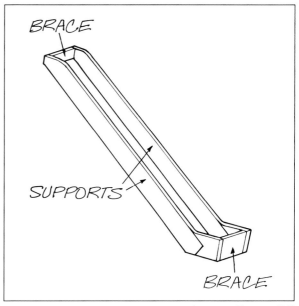

Figure CC

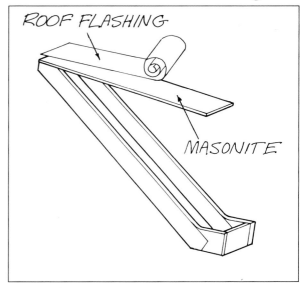

must be coutoured. Scale drawings for the contours are provided in **Figure FF**. Cut the contours on each piece according to the drawing.

7. The assembled slide frame (Support, Foot, and Brace pieces) is shown in **Figure BB**. To begin, attach a Brace between the Foot pieces, as shown. Attach one Support piece to each Foot, and nail the remaining Brace between the Supports at the opposite end, as shown in **Figure BB**.

8. Cut two 16-inch-wide strips of masonite, each 8 feet long. Carefully bend one piece over the curve at the upper end of the frame assembly and nail along the edges (**Figure CC**). Use as much of the remaining strip as necessary to complete the slide. Nail the metal roof flashing over the masonite, as shown.

Figure DD

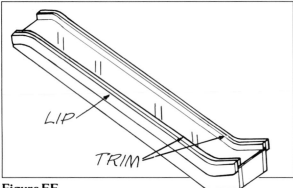

LIP

TRIM

9. Attach one Lip piece on each side of the frame assembly, as shown in **Figure DD**. Attach one Trim piece to the Lip on each side of the slide so that it covers the nail heads, as shown in **Figure DD**.

10. Install the slide so that it leads down from the remaining opening, securing it by inserting two lag screws through the Collar into each support (**Figure EE**).

11. Rub wax paper on the slide to make it smooth and slick. You can repeat this procedure to keep the slide well seasoned. Car polish also works well—and the buffing comes naturally!

Figure EE

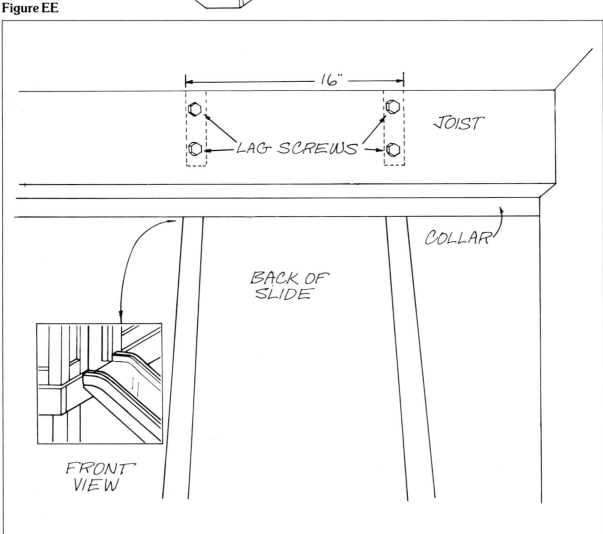

16"

JOIST

LAG SCREWS

COLLAR

BACK OF SLIDE

FRONT VIEW

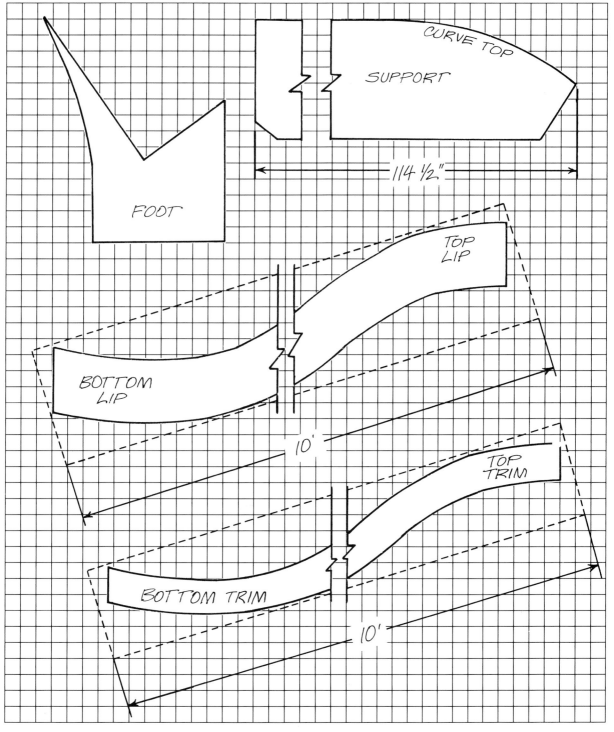

Variations on a Theme

Although the variations usually come after the theme, in this case it's best to consider them first. As we gathered ideas for our tree house, we soon became aware that the possibilities for this structure are almost limitless. And we're sure you'll have some ideas of your own. Just to get your imagination going, here are some examples of our ideas. All of the variations illustrated can be built using the basic plans provided in this book.

As you can see, we thought it best to leave the details up to our kid's imaginations. Why try to out-guess them? Keep it simple, and your tree house can be a fort, pirate ship, secret club room, castle, or jungle outpost.

Of course, the greatest part of creativity is being able to apply your ideas to the sometimes limited situation at hand. Your yard may not accommodate a tree house such as we've described, or as you've imagined. Just remember that nothing is cast in stone here – just adapt the basic structure to fit your situation, and see what alternatives present themselves. Remember that, and you won't find yourself "treed."

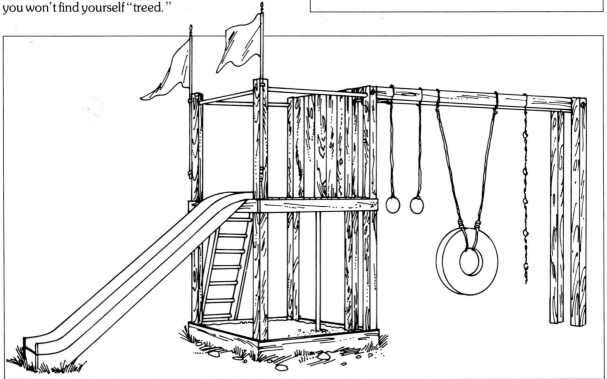

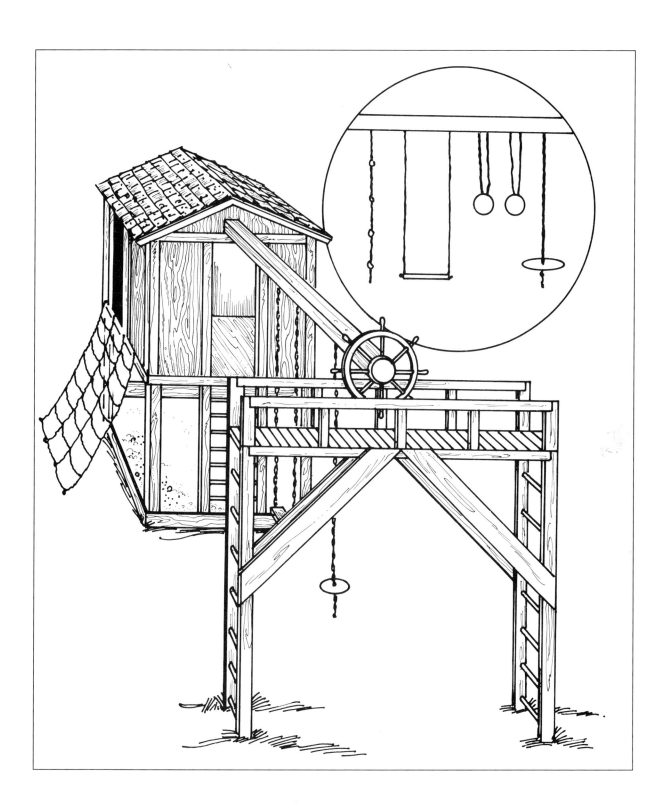

FREESTANDING TREE HOUSE

Modular Decking

Designing your own outdoor decking can be a nightmare of building codes, permits, and stress factors. If you thought putting in your own decking was just a matter of nailing a good sized chunk o' wood to a fair length o' lumber you have got another think coming to you - unless you are thinking of modular decking. This modular design makes it possible to build a complete deck in one weekend. The sections are light enough to be moved by one person to completely redesign the deck layout for a special party or a new flower bed.

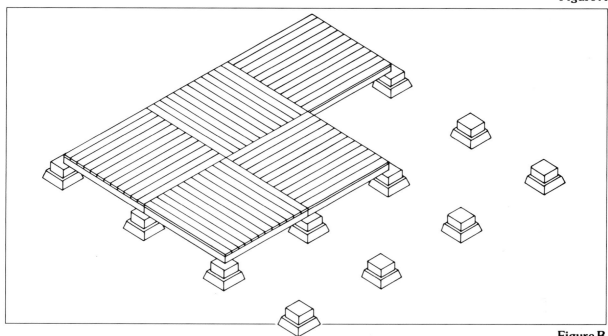

Materials

The following list is for one 4 x 4-foot module. Decide how many modules you will need to cover the desired area and multiply each of the materials listed below.

48 linear feet of 1 x 4 redwood
23 linear feet of 2 x 4 redwood
Twenty-four 10d common nails (minimum)
Fourty-eight 4d common nails (minimum)

Cutting the Wood

Cut the following pieces for one module:

Part	Material	Length	Quantity
Beams	2 x 4	48 inches	2
Joists	2 x 4	45 inches	4
Decking	1 x 4	48 inches	12

Footings

With a modular design, the placement of the footings is crucial. Plan out the area to be covered and carefully measure the exact distances between the footings (see **Figure A**).

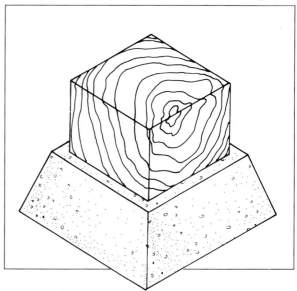

See the Tips & Techniques section on setting posts and footings. Use a line level to insure that the tops of all the piers are on the same level.

Because each pier is shared by as many as four deck modules, be sure to make them an adequate size (see **Figure B**).

Figure C

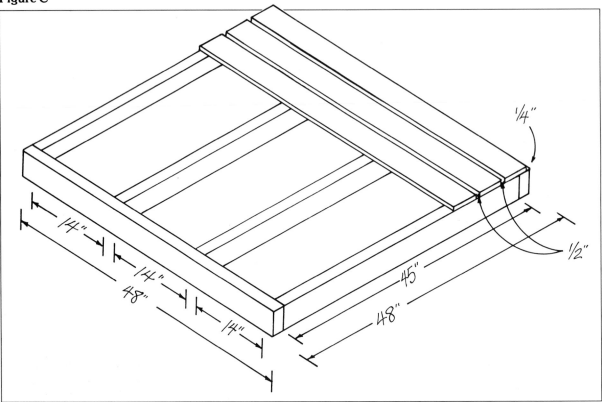

Figure D

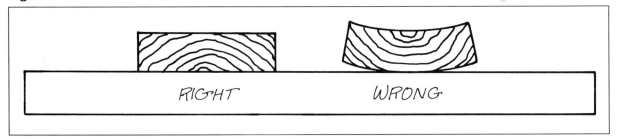

RIGHT   WRONG

Assembly

Refer to **Figure C** as you build the individual decking modules.

1. The joists are butted between the beams, with all pieces set on edge. Nail each joist in place allowing a 14-inch space between each two joists.

2. The decking is nailed across the joists, starting ¼ inch in from the edge of the beam. When positioning the decking boards, take a close look at the end grain

(the ends of the boards). The decking should be laid bark side up (see **Figure D**) to prevent the board from cupping. Allow a ½-inch space between each decking board. This space will help retard rot by allowing drainage and air circulation.

3. Repeat Steps 1 and 2 to build as many deck modules as you need.

4. Place the modules on the footing piers in any configuration you desire.

Privacy Fencing

A privacy fence should be thought of as more than just a barricade to keep people and animals in or out of your yard. If that's all you want, you should consider barbed wire! Privacy fences can accent or compliment your home and landscape. In todays "fish-bowl" neighborhoods, a privacy fence can also give you a tremendous amount of mental and physical freedom in your home as well as your yard, blocking out unsightly views from your side and prying eyes from the other. ANYONE can put up a privacy fence! A hammer, saw, shovel, and carpenter's level are just about the only tools you need. Add a few wooden marking stakes and a ball of string, and you're in the fencing business.

PLANNING

Types of Fences

The type and style of fence you want is largely a matter of personal preference, but there are a few basics to consider: Deciding WHERE you are going to put a fence will dictate a great deal the types of fences available to you. A latticework fence is ideal for short spans around a patio, but won't last long in a location where the neighborhood kids will be climbing over it to retrieve their lost ball. A solid panel fence will keep prying eyes out of your pool area, but will also keep out refreshing summer breezes. Drive around your neighborhood and look at the various privacy fences already up. Then go home, pull a chair into the back yard, sit down and try to imagine those fences in your yard. Will the fence block a view that you do, or do not want eliminated? How will that look with your existing landscape and house design? You might even consider asking the owners of particular fences if they have any complaints about the type of fence or fencing material. Questions are free, and if somebody has to make a mistake, let it be somebody else!

Location

The two most common locations for privacy fencing are around a patio or along property lines. If you are fencing around a patio, you don't have anything to worry about as far as location. If, however, you're planning to run the fence along property lines, you will need to be a little more careful in your planning.

First, try to find existing property markers. These are usually pieces of steel bars driven into the ground at the corners of your property. If you can't find the original markers, you should consider having your property lines resurveyed, or at least come to a mutual understanding with your neighbors to avoid problems after the fence is built.

With the corners of your lot established, set stakes into the ground at least six inches INSIDE those corners, and run a taut string along the proposed route of your fence (**Figure A**). Measure the total distance and make a sketch of your property showing the planned fence line, including the position and width of any gates (**Figure B**).

Figure A

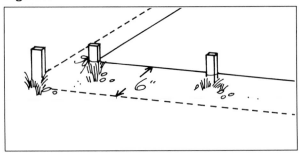

Figure B

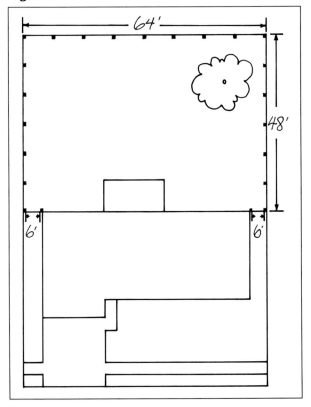

Material Requirements

When you have the type of fence selected and have measured the distance along the planned fence line, including gates, visit a local building materials supplier and he will be able to tell you how much fencing material you'll need for the number of planned feet, the recommended distance between posts, and how much the estimated total cost will be.

The size of and distance between posts depends greatly on your locale and the weight of the fence. A fairly standard distance between posts is 8 feet, using 4 x 4 posts. It is something of a tradeoff, dollar-wise, to use heavier but more expensive posts farther apart. Lightweight fencing, such as latticework, can be supported by lightweight posts at greater distances. An 8-foot-tall redwood fence may require 4 x 4 posts or heavier, set in concrete every 6 to 8 feet. Here in Oklahoma, where "the wind comes sweepin' down the plain" (and has been known to blow trucks off the road), a 6-foot-tall redwood fence requires a minimum of 4 x 4 posts set at 8-foot intervals.

Most dimensional lumber used for rails (the horizontal pieces extending between posts to which the fencing material is attached) comes in standard lengths of 4, 6, 8, and 10 feet. Careful positioning of the posts at one of these intervals can eliminate the need to cut the rail stock at all.

CONSTRUCTION

Posts and Rails

Measure out the intervals between posts along your proposed fence line and place a stake for each post, including gate posts, along the line. Remember to keep these stakes within YOUR property lines.

Once the locations of the posts are determined, you are ready to set them (see the Tips and Techniques section on setting posts and footings).

You are now ready to begin the actual assembly process. Note: If you have set your posts in concrete, allow

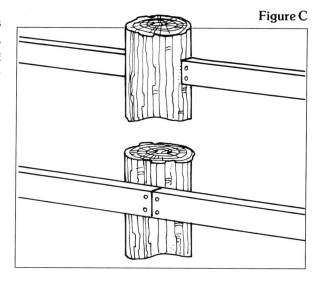

Figure C

them to stand for a week to ten days before proceeding so the concrete will have a chance to cure.

The next phase of construction is attaching the rails to the posts. This can be achieved in one of two ways: The rails can be butted against and toenailed to the posts, or they can overlap the posts (**Figure C**). Either method will work for the fences we have illustrated.

Very few yards are completely flat and level at all points. We will discuss two methods of adjusting your fence to compensate for the layout of your yard. Both methods begin with attaching the rails to the posts.

The Parallel Fence

With this method, the rails and the tops of the fence boards parallel the contours of your yard (**Figure D**).

Figure D

Figure E

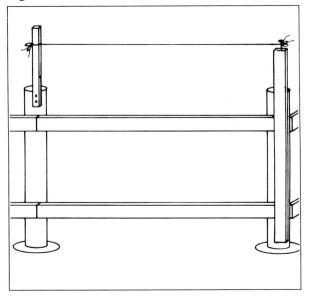

This method will work with any grade, but it will also make any rises and dips in your landscape even more obvious. If you buy pre-cut lengths of fencing material, this may be your only choice.

Figure F

1. The rails should run roughly 1 foot above ground level and 1 foot below the tops of your fence boards. Measure and make a mark 1 foot from either end of one fence board as a guide piece. Hold the guide piece against each post and mark each of them according to these marks.

2. Mount the rails to the posts at the points marked.

3. Start at one corner and place a fencing board against the rails, at least 1 inch off the ground. An easy way to achieve a consistent level is to drive a small nail into the top of the first fencing board mounted at the post, and then lightly tack a length of scrap wood to the top the next post (**Figure E**). Hold another piece of fencing in position against this post and mark the top of the board on the scrap wood. Now tie a string between the nail in the top of the first board and the marked level on the scrap piece. Each fencing board between the two posts can now be nailed in place with its top flush against the string. Use the carpenter's level to make sure each piece is true to vertical and nail in place. When you finish one section, pull the scrap piece from the post and repeat the process between the next two posts (**Figure E**).

The Stepped Fence

With this type of fence, the tops of the fencing boards are always true to horizontal, allowing occasional "steps" in the fence top to adjust the height to the grade of the land (**Figure F**). The amount of grade will determine the frequency of the steps you will need. This method can be used only if you are cutting your own fencing boards to length.

1. Start at the HIGHEST fence post and attach one end of the bottom rail approximately 1 foot above ground level. Use the carpenter's level to keep the rail horizontal and attach the opposite end of the rail to the next post.

2. Continue attaching rails in this manner until all the lower rails are in place. When the LOWEST point along the fence line is reached, reverse direction and attach the top rails. Measure from the ground up on each post to maintain the same distance between each set of top and bottom rails. Again, use the carpenter's level to keep the rails horizontal.

BUILDING OUTDOOR STRUCTURES

3. The biggest hassle about this type of fence is that every fence board must be measured to fit. Because the tops are always horizontal but the bottoms follow the contours of the land, every board will be a different length. To keep the tops of the fence boards flush place a piece of straight lumber over the fence boards mounted previously and extend the end over the next board top to be attached. Frequently use your carpenter's level on the top of the fence to make sure you aren't getting off level.

4. As you get to the stepped rails, adjust the height of the fence boards accordingly, returning to the height of the first fence board at the previous post.

5. With the fence boards in place, the next stage of the stepped fence is to frame the tops (this is actually an option, as the fence is complete without the frame). Start by measuring across the length of each stepped portion. Cut and mount 1 x 1s or 1 x 2s along both sides, flush with the top of the fence.

6. Cut and mount a 1 x 6 flat over the top of each stepped section.

7. At the stepped points, mount 1 bys and 1 x 6s in the same manner, running vertically only, and covering the vertical edge of the fence board.

Note: If your property is fairly level, this same process can be used to create a fence that has a perfectly horizontal framed top, without steps.

The Alternating Board Fence

One problem with most types of privacy fences is that one neighbor gets the nice flush side and the other gets the post and rail side. The alternating board fence solves this to some degree by facing every second fence board on opposite sides (**Figure G**). This fence also permits air to circulate through the fence.

1. For best appearance with the alternating board fence, use square fence posts the same width as the rails and the same height (from the ground) as the fence boards. Example: Use 4 x 4 square posts with 2 x 4 rails so the edges will be flush.

2. The rails for the alternating board fence are toenailed in place between the posts. If you don't want to cut the rails to fit, placement of the posts is crucial.

3. Tack a length of string flat to the top of each post and run to the top of the next post as a guide for the fence boards.

4. The fence boards will be attached to the rails AND posts with a space between each two boards on the same side, slightly less than the width of a fence board. If viewed from the top, the boards on alternating sides overlap slightly. To make a spacer, rip 2 inches from the full length of a spare fencing board. Use the remaining portion of the board as a spacer as you attach the fence boards on one side.

5. Repeat Step 4 for the opposite side, making sure that you are overlapping the boards mounted on the finished side.

The Latticework Fence

The latticework fence requires fewer and lighter-weight materials than any other type of fence. For the same reason, however, it is recommended chiefly for use in short spans where it will be the least subject to wind, weather, and people who like to climb fences! You should also remember that a lattice fence is only "semi-private," there being spaces between each lattice strip. If you get stuck with the post-and-rail side of another type of privacy fence, latticework panels make a nice cover-up and a great place to grow roses.

Figure G

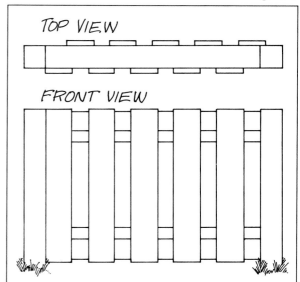

TOP VIEW

FRONT VIEW

Figure H

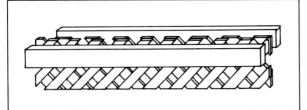

Figure I

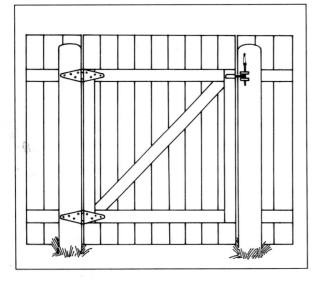

1. Rip ¼-inch-thick lattice strips using a table saw. If you don't have access to a table saw, most lumber yards will perform this task for a fee.

If you want lattice strips wider than 2 inches, simply cut them from wider lumber stock. We discovered that lattice wider than 2 inches is harder to work with, however, as it tends to split and warp unless it is cut much thicker than ¼ inch.

2. Assembly of a latticework fence is really a snap, especially if you have a good heavy-duty staple gun. The lattice is sandwiched diagonally between two top and two bottom 1 x 4 rails (**Figure H**). Begin by measuring each post and marking the desired position of the top and the bottom of the fence. Unlike the other fences we've discussed, the rails for a latticework fence are at the very top and bottom of the fence.

3. Nail the first layer of rails, top and bottom parallel to each other, overlapping the posts.

4. Attach the first lattice strip diagonally between the bottom corner at one end of the fence and the top corner formed by the next post and rail.

5. Use a piece of stock the same width as the lattice as a spacer between strips and continue mounting full-length strips until the other end of the fence is reached.

6. To fill in the corners, you will need to set the spacer and measure for each remaining lattice strip.

7. Now reverse the direction of the lattice, repeating the procedures above to attach a second layer of lattice strips to the 1 x 4 rails.

8. With all of the lattice strips in place, nail the second layer of 1 x 4 rails over the latticework, parallel and flush with the first set of rails.

9. 1 x 4s can now be mounted horizontally over the tops of the rails, if so desired.

Gates

Gates generally will be subjected to more wear-and-tear than the rest of your fence. Because of this, extra care should be taken in building the gate and in selecting hardware to mount it on the fence.

1. There must be a post on either side of the gate. Even if none of the rest of them are, these gate posts should be set in concrete. This must be planned for in advance when laying out the boundaries of the fence. Refer to **Figure I** as you build the gate.

2. The first step in building the gate itself is constructing a support frame to keep the gate from sagging. Measure the distance between rails on the fence and the distance between gate posts – both at the top and the bottom of the gate opening. Construct a frame 1 inch narrower than the gate opening. Add a diagonal brace inside the frame and attach it to all four sides of the frame at the corners.

3. Attach the fence boards to the frame, with the tops of the fence boards extending past the top of the frame the same distance that the fence boards extend beyond the fence rails.

4. Attach the hinges to the gate frame.

5. Brace the gate in position and attach the hinges to the posts.

6. The gate latch will be attached to the other side of the frame. Depending on the type of latch you purchased, portions of the gate and/or post may need to be trimmed for latch clearance.

Privy Storage Shed

The old standard now serves the important function of keeping all your outdoor gardening equipment. This classic model is approximately 5 feet square and 8 feet high. Covered with rough cedar siding, it's a natural with wooden decking.

Figure A

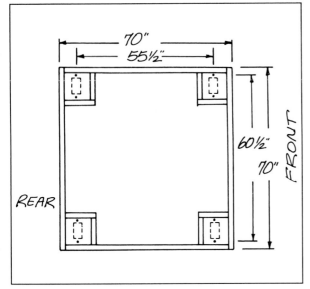

Figure B

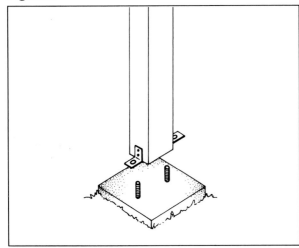

Figure C

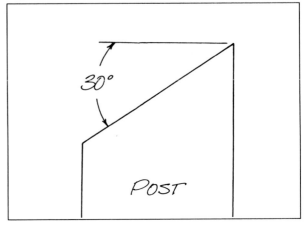

Two 4 x 8-foot sheets of ½-inch waferwood or exterior plywood
Tarpaper and shingles
Four floor joist hangers
Three exterior spring-loaded door hinges
Eight L-brackets, eight bolts, each 6 inches long, washers, and nuts
8d and 3d galvanized nails
Four bags of cement for footings

Building the Footings

A 4 x 6 cedar post located at each corner of the privy supports the structure. The posts are spaced as shown in **Figure A**. Build four level footings spaced to accommodate the posts (see the Tips & Techniques section).

While the concrete is still wet, set two threaded bolts upright into each footing (**Figure B**), so that L-brackets attached to the posts will fit down over the bolts. The L-brackets are attached on either side of the 4 x 6 cedar posts so that the posts can then be fastened securely on top of the footings using washers and nuts.

We built the privy into the decking near our pool, so we wanted the floor to be even with the decking. If you're using this arrangement, calculate the length of the posts by measuring from the ground to the top of your decking, then add 76½ inches for the two rear posts, and 93½ inches for the two front posts. **Note:** If your decking is less than 6 inches above the ground, each post will need to be a bit longer, because of the width of the floor joists.

Materials

250 linear feet of 6-inch-wide lap-and-gap cedar siding
35 linear feet of rough cedar 4 x 6
90 linear feet of redwood 2 x 6
180 linear feet of redwood 2 x 4
25 linear feet of redwood 2 x 2
30 linear feet of rough cedar 1 x 8
100 linear feet of redwood 1 x 4
30 linear feet of redwood 1 x 2

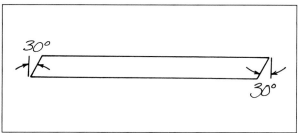

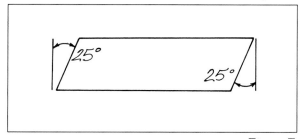

Figure F

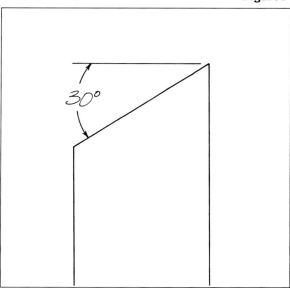

Framing the Floor, Walls, and Roof

1. Bevel the upper end of each corner post at a 30-degree angle, as shown in **Figure C**. Stand the posts and secure each one to its footing.

2. Cut the pieces listed below from redwood 2 x 6. Label each piece with its code letter as indicated.

Code	Length	Quantity
A	48 inches	2
B	52 inches	4
C	56½ inches	2

3. Cut and label the pieces listed below from redwood 2 x 4.

Code	Length	Quantity
D	72½ inches	4
E	70 inches	4
F	62½ inches	2
G	60 inches	2
H	19 inches	9
I	5 inches	4
J	7 inches	6
K	84 inches	2
L	77 inches	2
M	92 inches	2
N	73 inches	3

Figure G

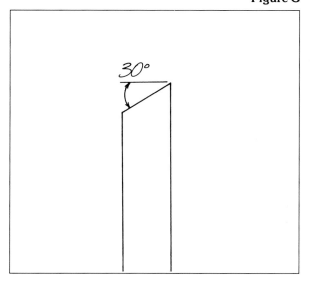

4. Miter both ends of each D, F, and I piece at a 30-degree angle, as shown in **Figure D**. In addition, miter both ends of each J piece at a 25-degree angle, as shown in **Figure E**. Miter one end of each K and L piece at a 30-degree angle, as shown in **Figure F**. Bevel one end of each M and N piece at a 30-degree angle, as shown in **Figure G**.

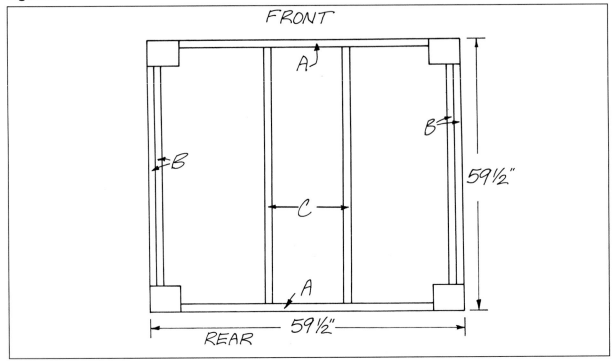

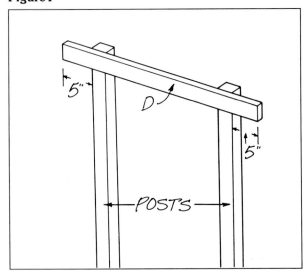

Figure I

B pieces between the posts as shown. Attach each **C** piece between the **A** pieces as shown using a joist hanger at each end. Space the **C** pieces so they won't interfere with any plumbing you're planning to install.

6. The assembled roof frame is shown in **Figure J**. To begin, nail one **D** piece to a front and back Post, so that the upper edge is flush with the tops of the Posts. Allow 5 inches to extend beyond the Post on each end (**Figure I**). Nail another **D** piece to the opposite Posts in the same manner. Nail one **E** piece across the front ends of the **D** pieces, with 5 inches extending beyond the **D** piece on each end, as shown in **Figure J**. Nail another **E** piece across the rear ends of the **D** pieces in the same manner. Nail an additional **D** piece between the **E** pieces on each side, flush with the ends, as shown. Nail the **F**, **G**, **H**, and **I** pieces to the frame as shown in **Figure J**.

5. The assembled floor frame is shown in **Figure H**. The upper edges of all pieces in the floor frame are 92 inches below the top of the front posts, and 75 inches below the top of the rear posts. To begin, nail the **A** and

7. To build the front porch overhang, construct a frame using **E** and **J** pieces, as shown in **Figure J**. Nail the assembled frame to the front **E** piece of the roof frame (**Figure J**).

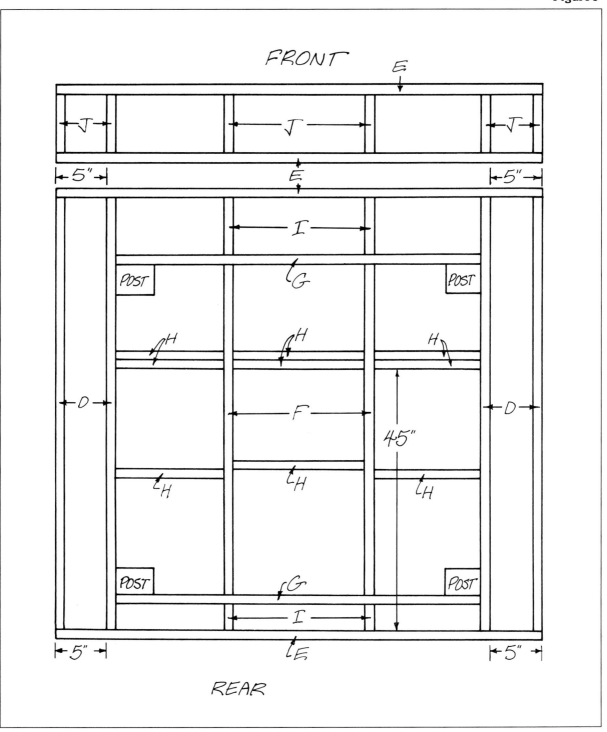

Figure J

FRONT

REAR

Figure K

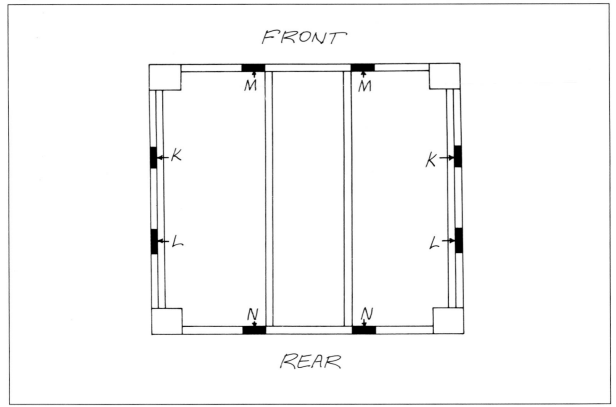

Figure L

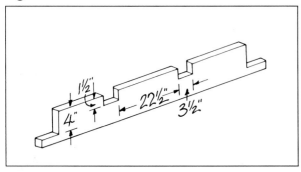

8. Nail the wall studs (K, L, M, and N pieces) to the floor frame (A and B pieces) and roof frame (D and E pieces), as shown in **Figure K**. The upper ends of all studs should be even with the upper edges of the roof frame pieces.

9. To create the floor, cut lengths of redwood 2 x 6 to fit across the floor joists. These floor boards rest on the inner B pieces that run along each side of the floor frame. A cutting diagram for the notches in the front floor board is provided in **Figure L**. The end notches will accommodate the Posts, and those in the middle will accommodate the wall studs. Cut the notches in the front board, and install the floor boards as shown in **Figure M**. For the rear floor board, cut notches in the ends only. To fill the gap between the floor boards and the side walls, rip approximately 6 feet of 2 x 4 in half. Cut lengths to fit between the wall studs along the ends of the floor boards.

10. To build the front step, cut two lengths of redwood 2 x 4, each 14½ inches long. In addition, cut one 61-inch length of 2 x 4. Nail the three lengths together to make a frame against the front posts of the privy, as shown in **Figure N**. Nail the frame to the front posts, as illustrated. Cut three lengths of redwood 2 x 6, each 61 inches long, and nail them to the frame as shown.

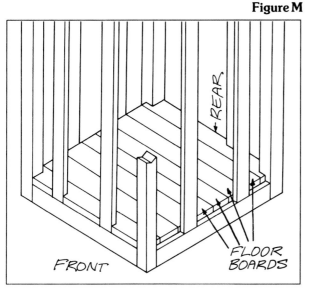

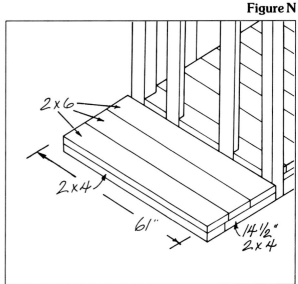

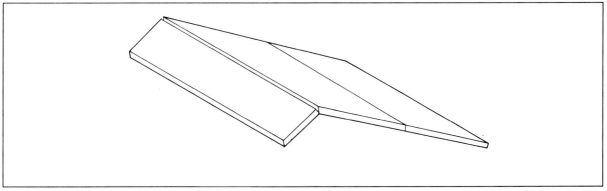

Covering the Roof

1. Cut three pieces of ½-inch waferwood or exterior plywood to cover the roof. Butt the edges along the long slope and peak as shown in **Figure O**.

2. Cut trim pieces from rough cedar 1 x 8 to fit around the roof, as shown in **Figure P**. Miter the pieces to fit neatly at the corners.

3. Cut trim pieces from rough cedar 1 x 2 to fit over the trim you installed in Step 2. Install this trim as shown in **Figure P**, mitering the ends so they fit neatly at the corners.

4. Lay tarpaper and shingle the roof (see the Tips & Techniques section for roofing pointers).

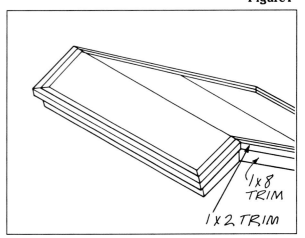

Figure Q

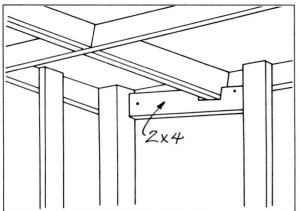

Figure S

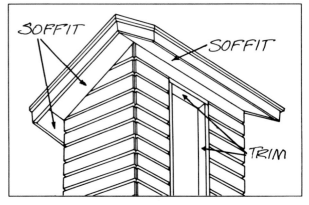

Figure R

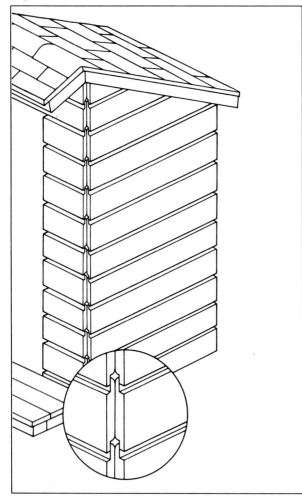

Attaching the Soffit, Siding, and Trim

1. Before you attach the siding, cut several lengths of 2 x 4 to fit between the side wall studs, as shown in **Figure Q**. Nail these pieces along the roof frame pieces on each side, as shown in **Figure Q**, allowing approximately 1½ inches to extend below the lower edge of the frame piece.

2. Cut lengths of siding to fit along each side of the privy. Each side will take eleven or twelve lengths to cover. On two sides of the privy, miter the upper lengths at a 30-degree angle so they fit against the roof, as shown in **Figure R**. Install the siding beginning at the bottom of each side and working to the top, overlapping the edges as shown.

3. Cut one piece of waferwood or exterior plywood to fit as a soffit under the front eaves, as shown in **Figure S**. This soffit piece should be installed level, not sloping at the roof pitch. Cut another piece of waferwood to fit as a soffit under the back eaves, and install it as shown in **Figure S**. Cut two more pieces and install them along the side eaves, butting the ends as shown in **Figure S**.

4. Cut trim pieces from rough cedar 1 x 4 to fit around the doorway opening, as shown in **Figure S**. Install the trim as illustrated, nailing the pieces even with the wall studs and roof frame.

5. Cut trim pieces from rough cedar 1 x 4 to fit under the soffits and around the bottom of the privy. Install the trim as shown in **Figure T**.

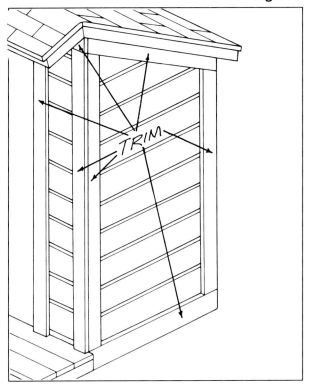

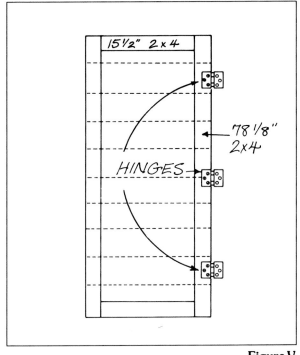

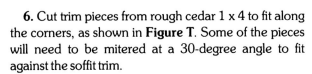

Figure V

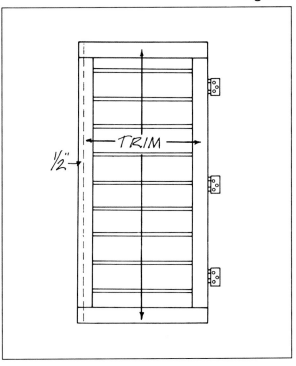

6. Cut trim pieces from rough cedar 1 x 4 to fit along the corners, as shown in **Figure T**. Some of the pieces will need to be mitered at a 30-degree angle to fit against the soffit trim.

Building the Door

1. Cut two lengths of redwood 2 x 4, each 78⅛ inches long. Cut two additional lengths of 2 x 4, each 15½ inches long.

2. Nail the four lengths of 2 x 4 together to make a frame, as shown in **Figure U**. Nail twelve lengths of cedar siding to the frame, as shown.

3. Install three spring-loaded hinges along one side of the door, attaching them to the siding as shown in **Figure U**. Be sure the screws go into the frame.

4. Cut trim pieces from rough cedar 1 x 4 to fit around the face of the door, as shown in **Figure V**. Attach the trim to the door siding, so that one long piece extends ½ inch beyond one side (this piece serves as a doorstop).

Figure W

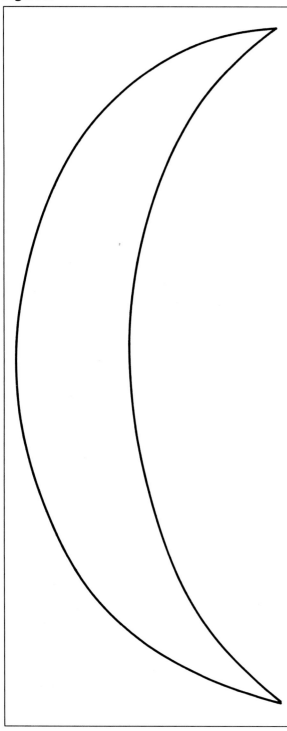

Figure X

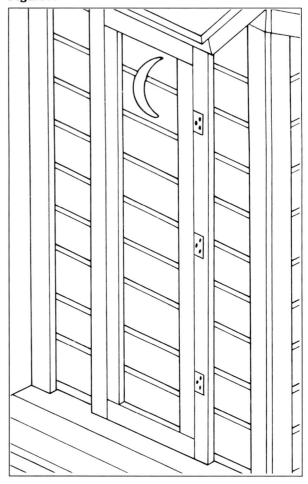

5. A full-size pattern for the famous crescent moon is provided in **Figure W**. Transfer the pattern to the upper two pieces of door siding, and cut it out using a portable jig or keyhole saw.

6. Hang the door by attaching the hinges to the trim pieces around the doorway, as shown in **Figure X**.

Building the Porch Railing

1. Cut the pieces listed below from redwood 2 x 4.

Code	Length	Quantity
O	12¾ inches	2
P	22 inches	2
Q	33½ inches	2

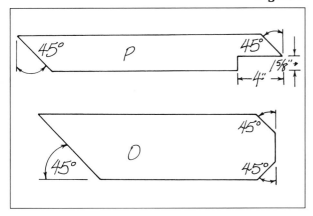

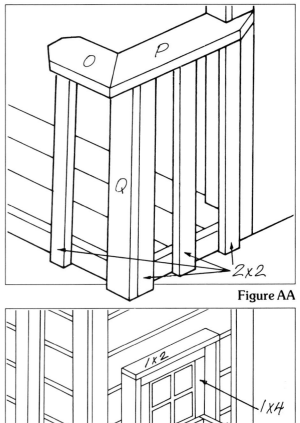

2. Cut eight lengths of redwood 2 x 2, each 33½ inches long.

3. Miter one end of each O and P piece at a 45-degree angle, as shown in **Figure Y**. In addition, miter the opposite end of each P piece at a 45-degree angle and cut a 1⅝ x 4-inch notch, as shown in **Figure Y**. Miter the opposite end of each O piece (**Figure Y**).

4. One assembled railing is shown in **Figure Z**. To begin, nail one length of 2 x 2 to the trim at the front of the privy, as shown. Nail the P piece to the 2 x 2 and privy as shown, then nail three additional lengths of 2 x 2 to the P piece. Nail the O piece to the P piece, and nail a Q piece under the corner, as shown. Nail the remaining length of 2 x 2 under the opposite end of the O piece, as shown.

5. Build an identical railing at the opposite front corner of the privy.

Building the Window Planter

1. Cut a 16-inch-square piece of ½-inch waferwood or exterior plywood to serve as the window "panes." Nail this piece to one side of the privy.

2. Rip eight 16-inch lengths of trim, ⅜ inch wide, from any remaining 1 x 2 or 1 x 4 boards. Cut the lengths to fit around the waferwood window pane, as shown in **Figure AA**. Cut notches in the middle of the two remaining lengths, and nail them to the waferwood pane, as shown.

3. Cut four trim pieces from rough cedar 1 x 4 to fit around the window, and nail them in place, as shown in **Figure AA**.

4. To build the planter box, rip approximately 3 feet of rough cedar 1 x 8 down to a 5-inch width. From this, cut two 5-inch lengths for the ends of the planter, and one 23½-inch length for the planter front. Nail the pieces at the lower edge of the window, as shown in **Figure AA**. Cut a floor piece for the planter and nail it between the ends.

5. Cut three lengths of rough cedar 1 x 2 to fit around the top and sides of the window and planter, as shown in **Figure AA**. Nail these pieces to the edges of the 1 x 4 trim, as illustrated.

Gazebo Party Center

At the turn of the century, wide verandas, summer evenings on the porch swing, lemonade, and gazebos supplied the laid-back atmosphere for the family at leisure. You can recapture some of that time and simple pleasure with this handsome and functional gazebo party center.

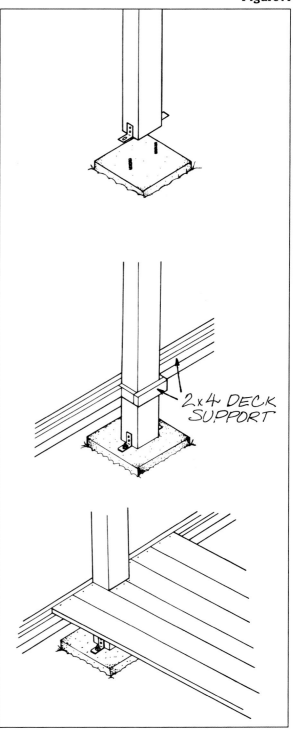

Don't let the size of the project scare you; it's amazingly simple to construct and has a wide variety of options that can reflect your own needs and imagination.

The first step in this plan is to get a glass of lemonade, step into your back yard, close your eyes and imagine a warm summer evening with your family and friends. The rest of the project is almost as easy.

Our gazebo is twelve feet square although these plans can be utilized for any size you wish. We chose a latticework half-wall, leaving one side open for a serving bar into our pool area. Inside we constructed a built-in barbeque pit, vented through the cupola. Throughout this project we'll discuss other suggested options, but one quick read through the instructions and you're sure to visualize a few of your own.

The Footings

Visualize where and what size you want your gazebo to be. Mark out the boundries with stakes and string. How's it look so far? Once you're satisfied that you have the gazebo positioned where you want it and the corners are square and true, you may wish to remove the sod from the area the gazebo will cover. Moving the sod isn't absolutely necessary but if you have any bare spots elsewhere in your yard it won't be wasted and besides, grass growing up between the decking has never been one our favorite things.

As we said, our gazebo is twelve feet to a side. Our footings are twelve-inch-square concrete, set two feet into the ground (see the Tips and Techniques section) at four-foot intervals around the perimeter and across as support for the floor joists (see **Figure C**). While our concrete was still wet we set two threaded bolts upright into each footing (see **Figure A**), so that L-brackets attached to the posts would fit down over the bolts.

The L-brackets are attached on either side of our 4 x 6 redwood posts so that the posts can then be fastened securely atop the footings using washers and nuts to fit. Redwood, for all its strength and beauty, will eventually rot when set into concrete and using this method makes it easier to measure and set the posts.

These posts support the entire structure and deck so

Figure B

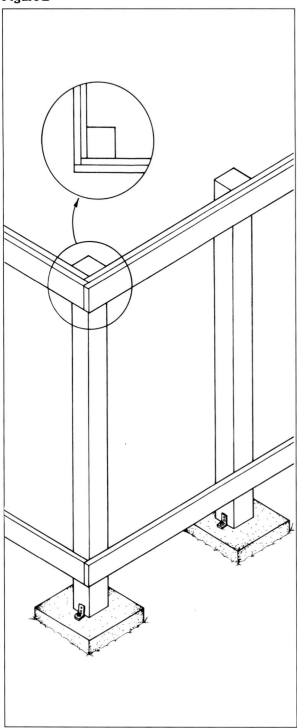

take your time and make sure the posts are aligned and the corners square. If your building site isn't level, your posts will have to be varied in length to compensate for the drop or rise or, if the change in grade isn't drastic, the footings can be built up to level – the tops of the posts must all be at the same overall height or your roof will lean, putting uneven stress on the posts and eventually pulling over the entire structure.

When selecting your building materials take this stress into account. It is best to use at least 4 x 4 posts, and if the deck is to be elevated over a few feet you should consider even larger posts such as 4 x 6 and placing them no more than four feet apart.

The Collars

Attached to the outside of our posts, flush with the tops and again near the bottom (deck level), we girdled our structure with 2 x 6 redwood collars (see **Figure B**). These collars support the floor joists and the rafters (called the plate) so make sure both are level and parallel. To add extra support for the roof we next attached an outer collar of 2 x 6-inch redwood around the 2 x 6 top collar already in place.

You may not feel that this added support is necessary, but we did not use joists in the roof framing and without substantial collar support the weight of the roof will tend to push the walls apart. If you want your gazebo to last forever, attach the collars to the posts using recessed bolts or lag bolts.

The Floor Joists

If you are planning to install a built-in barbeque this is the time to start before you install the floor joists. See the Tips and Techniques section of this book for proper methods of building a brick barbeque. There's a little more to it than just laying brick unless you're fond of barbequed gazebo. **Figure C** shows our barbeque in place with the head-ups (altering the normal course of the joists) necessary to support the decking around it.

Putting the floor joists in at this time adds more rigidity to your structure before starting on the roof. Here, again, we used 2 x 6-inch redwood.

You'll find metal joist hangers to be the greatest invention since sliced bread. If you want your decking to

Figure C

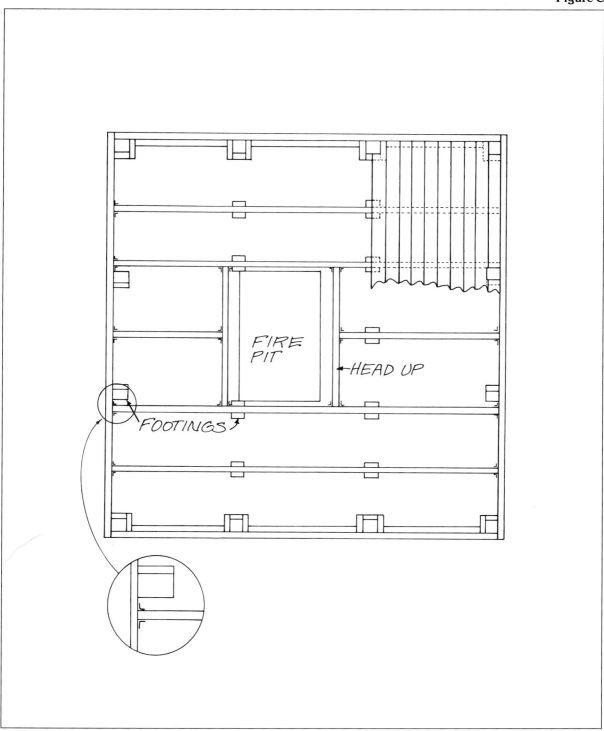

FIRE PIT

←HEAD UP

FOOTINGS↗

Figure D

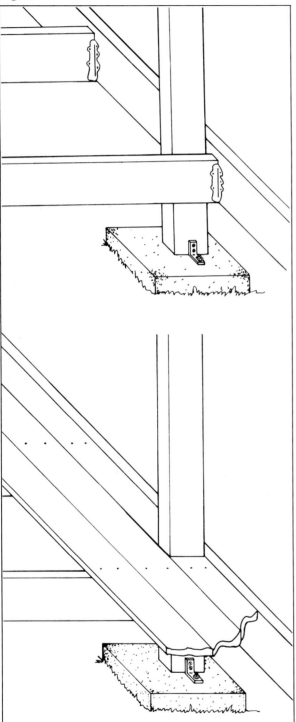

be flush with the top of the lower collar, measure the thickness of the decking material and attach the joists that distance below the top edge of the collar (see **Figure D**). The floor joists are then mounted every two feet and a head-up built around the barbeque.

To support the decking at either end of the gazebo, parallel to the joists, we mounted 2 x 4-inch supports to the collar frame so that the tops of the supports were at the same level as the tops of the joists (see **Figure A**). It was necessary to build a box around each post to insure that the ends of the decking would be completely supported at all points.

The Decking

For decking material we used 1 x 6-inch redwood. We hate to stress the obvious, but the decking is nailed ACROSS the floor joists as in **Figures A** and **D** (we don't want anybody claiming we left anything out). If you didn't quite get your structure perfectly square (we didn't) the last piece of decking will have to be trimmed to fit.

The material you use for your decking, and the pattern that you install it in, are other options available to you. Before you get too creative though, remember the decking must be fully supported from underneath.

The Rafters

This is undoubtedly the toughest part of the entire project. When this one is licked, you have a gazebo! Everything else is just trim. Hoping that our rafters would always remain dry, we used #2 yellow pine instead of expensive redwood.

The first problem is figuring the pitch of the roof and the length of the rafters. This roof design requires three different types of rafters: common, hip, and hip jack. **Figure E** shows the formulas used for calculating the length of these rafters from the peak (the cupola) to the plate (the top collar). We added twelve inches to these lengths for the foot of each rafter (the eave).

The Rise – For our gazebo we decided on an 8/12 cut, or eight inches of rise for every twelve inches of run (the level distance over which the rafter will run). Using the formula in **Figure E** we see that we must first find the run, or the LEVEL distance from the plate to the peak. Our structure is twelve feet wide and subtracting the width of the cupola, or two feet, we know that the

CALCULATING RISE AND RAFTER LENGTH

Rise

Rise = ratio x run

example: using a 8/12 ratio and a run of 5-feet

8-inches x 5-feet = 40-inches or 3.3-feet

Rafter Lengths

Common Rafter Length $= \sqrt{run^2 + rise^2}$

example: using a calculated rise of 3.3-feet and a run of 5-feet

$\sqrt{5^2 + 3.3^2} = \sqrt{25 + 10.8} = \sqrt{35.8} = 6$-feet (top to plate)

Hip Rafter Length $= \sqrt{run^2 + plate\ length^2}$

(note: plate length is the distance between the hip rafter and the common rafter)

example: using a run of 5-feet and a plate length of 5-feet

$\sqrt{5^2 + 5^2} = \sqrt{25 + 25} = \sqrt{50} = 7$-feet (common to plate)

Hip Jack Rafter Length =

$$\frac{(common\ rafter\ length)}{(number\ of\ spaces\ between\ common\ rafter\ and\ end)} = difference$$

then

(common rafter length) − difference = first hip jack length

then

(first hip jack length) − difference = second hip jack length

example: using a common rafter length of 6 feet and the number of spaces = 2.5
(the last space is half the first)

$$\frac{6}{2.5} = 2.4 \text{ (difference)}$$

then

6 − 2.4 = 3.6 (length of first hip jack rafter)

then

3.6 − 2.4 = 1.2 (length of second hip jack rafter)

Note: All lengths are rounded to the nearest tenth foot.

Figure F

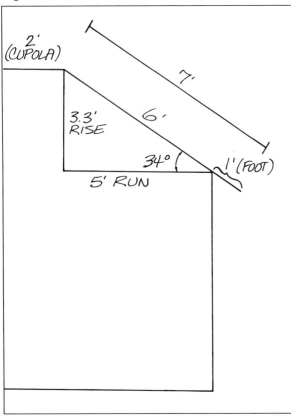

Figure G

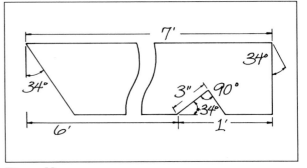

Figure H

Table of Roof Slope Ratio to Foot Angle

Roof Slope	Foot Angle	Roof Slope	Foot Angle
1/12	5°	7/12	31°
2/12	10°	8/12	34°
3/12	15°	9/12	37°
4/12	19°	10/12	40°
5/12	23°	11/12	43°
6/12	27°	12/12	45°

span is ten feet and the run is half that or five feet refer to **Figure F**.

Since we know that there will be eight inches of rise for every one foot of run, we can calculate the rise as being 8 (inches) times 5 (feet) equals 40(inches) or 3.3-feet of rise.

Common Rafters – To calculate the length of the common rafters we use the formula shown in **Figure E**. Using the known run and rise, we find that our common rafters should be 6 feet from the peak to the plate, plus 1 foot for the foot, or 7 feet in total length.

The top cut and seat cut for the common rafters are shown in **Figure G**. These rafter cuts are correct for our twelve- by-twelve-foot structure with a roof cut of 8/12, if you have changed either of these factors the lengths and angles of cuts will be different. The table in **Figure H** shows the degree of angle for various roof slopes per 12 inches of run. Example: We are using an 8/12 roof

cut, which corresponds to a 34-degree slope. This then is the proper angle to use in our rafter cuts.

Mark on the plate the positions your rafters will take. The rafters will seat (where the rafter and the plate intersect) one foot from each corner and every two feet thereafter.

Our roof framing begins with a 2 x 2-foot box made from 2 x 6-inch lumber (see **Figure I**) and reenforced with diagonal braces. These braces insure that the box, and so the roof itself, remain square during construction. Once the roof is finished the braces can be removed from the box.

To this box nail four of the common rafters, two on each of opposite faces. Have someone help you lift this assembly into position and secure it to the plate.

Attach the remaining common rafters to the box and plate, two to a side on the remaining two sides.

Hip Rafters – The hip rafters run from the corners of the plate and attach to the common rafters just below the box. A formula for calculating the length of the hip rafters is supplied in **Figure E**.

Because the hip rafters are mounted in the corners,

Figure I

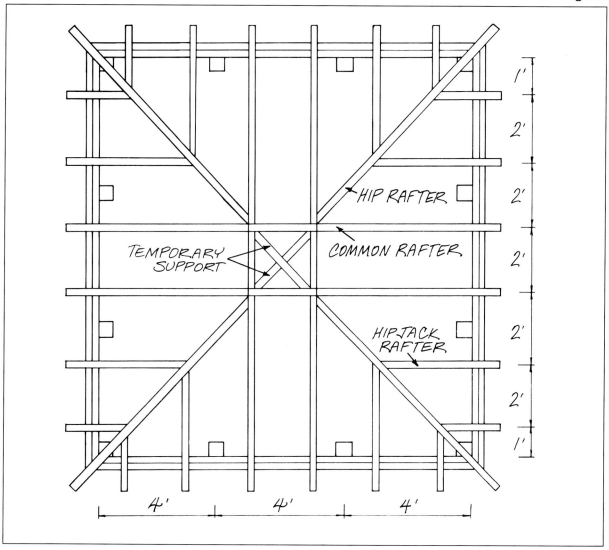

they require not only the top cut but also a 45-degree cheek or side cut to connect with the common rafters (see **Figure J**). The seat cut extends over the plate and the corner post as well, so depending on the dimensions of your post, make this cut accordingly.

Attach the hip rafters to the common rafters as shown in **Figure J**, seating them across the corner posts.

Hip Jack Rafters – The hip jack rafters run parallel to the common rafters, seated at two foot intervals at the plate and joining against the hip rafter at 45-degree an-

gles (see **Figure I**). The top cut for these rafters is the same as for the hip rafters, having a top cut and a cheek, or side cut (refer to **Figure J**). The seat cut is the same as for the common rafters (**Figure G**).

The formula in **Figure E** shows how to calculate the length of your hip jack rafters.

Attach the hip jack rafters parallel to the common rafters with the top cut butting against the hip rafters and the seat cut at the plate.

The last step in the roof framing process is building

Figure J

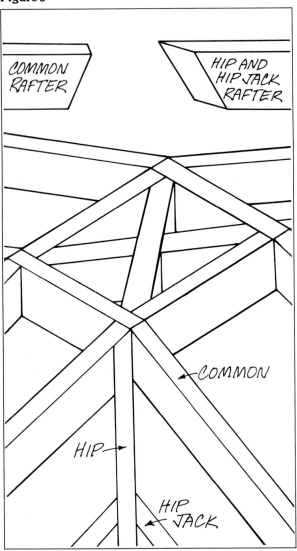

COMMON RAFTER

HIP AND HIP JACK RAFTER

COMMON

HIP

HIP JACK

Figure K

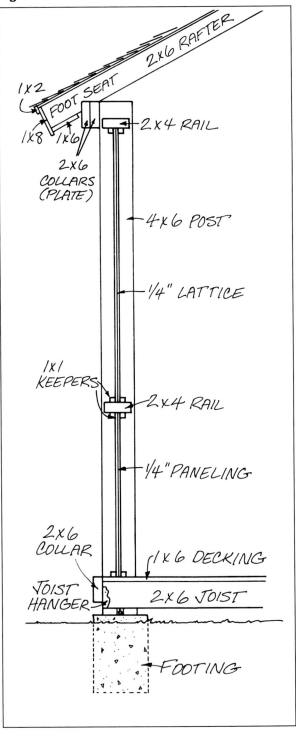

1X2

FOOT SEAT

2X6 RAFTER

1X8 1X6

2X6 COLLARS (PLATE)

2X4 RAIL

4X6 POST

1/4" LATTICE

1X1 KEEPERS

2X4 RAIL

1/4" PANELING

2X6 COLLAR

JOIST HANGER

1X6 DECKING

2X6 JOIST

FOOTING

a box around the foot of the rafters (see **Figure K**). Redwood 1 x 6 is used under the eaves, flush with the ends of the rafters, and redwood 1 x 8 is used across the ends of the rafters flush at the top. An additional 1 x 2-inch piece of redwood is mounted over the top of the 1 x 8-inch board with its upper edge protruding ¼ inch above the rafter. This insures that runoff from the roof does not seep back between the plywood and the shingles, and also gives added support to the plywood which butts against it.

Figure L

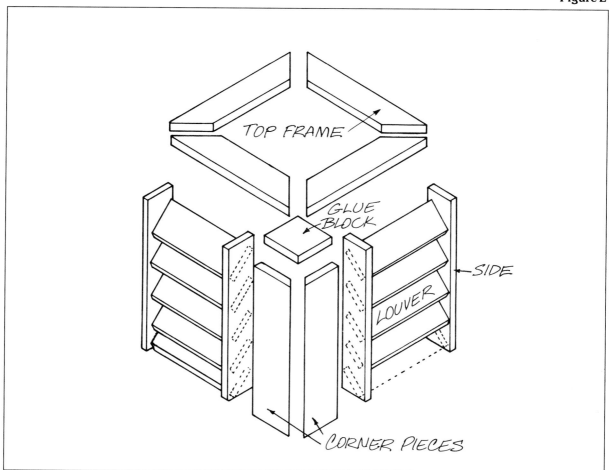

TOP FRAME

GLUE BLOCK

SIDE

LOUVER

CORNER PIECES

You're now ready to attach the plywood roof sheeting, roofing felt, and shingles as described in the Tips and Techniques section. The cupola, which is discussed next, is attached to the peak after the roof has been shingled.

The Cupola

The cupola serves not only as decoration but also as the vent for the barbeque. Ours is basically just a two-foot louvered cube with a peaked roof matching that of the gazebo. This is not structurally important so you may build your cupola in any size or shape or leave it out altogether; just make sure you compensate your roofing plans accordingly.

The louvers are assembled in four seperate panels (**Figure L**) and all parts are cut from 1 x 4 redwood. The louvers are 15½ inches long and the sides to which the louvers are attached are 2 feet in length. The four top pieces form a two-foot-square (inside dimensions) mitered frame. Small 3 x 3-inch glue blocks are positioned between the louver panels to support the 2-foot-long corner pieces, which are given mitered joining edges.

Thankfully, the roof for the cupola is not nearly as complicated as the gazebo roof. You simply cut four triangular pieces of plywood, each 3 feet across the base and 2½ feet on the remaining two sides. The four cupola roof panels are joined using short lengths of 1 x 1-inch wood strips (see **Figure M**).

Figure M

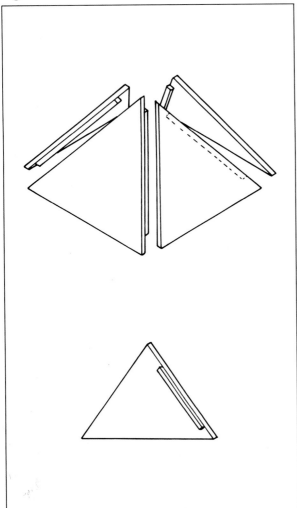

Figure N

COPPER
STRIPS

With the cupola roof assembled, simply position it over the louver panels and nail in place to the top frame. Cover the roof with roofing felt and shingles (see Tips & Techniques).

Before putting the cupola in place, we attached 1-foot-wide x 2-foot-long copper strips to the opening in the gazebo roof. It is not absolutely necessary that you use copper, but it must be something that will properly shed water and not rust. These strips extend both inward and outward past the base of the cupola to insure that water will not come into the gazebo or seep under the top edge of the shingles (**Figure N**).

The cupola can now be positioned and toe-nailed (see Tips & Techniques section) into place atop the gazebo roof.

The Wall Panels

This is another of those areas that is open to your imagination. You may wish to screen in your gazebo, use glass panels, or leave it completely open. For our plans, we chose to use rough cedar paneling on the bottom one-third and open latticework above. Installing this type of walling is VERY simple. Refer to **Figure K** as you install these panels.

To begin with, we butted 2 x 4-inch redwood rails between our posts: one at the top, flush with the bottom of the 4 x 6-inch plate; and another, parallel with the first, 30 inches above the deck level. These were secured to the posts by toe-nailing them into position.

The individual openings between the rails can now be measured and the panels pre-fabricated.

Two ¼-inch rough cedar panels are cut to size to fit between posts and between the rail and deck. These panels are installed in pairs, back to back, to resist warping or bowing.

The latticework is made from 2-inch-wide strips cut from the same ¼-inch rough cedar paneling used for the solid panels. The lattice panels can be made in a continous sheet by overlapping 6-foot strips at an angle that will allow them to span the space between posts along the diagonal. A scrap piece of 4-inch-wide wood can be used as a template to keep the strips parallel, and an occasional brad is all that's needed to secure the pieces together. When you have enough of the latticework completed, you can trim the sides to the appropriate width and cut lengths of the latticework to fit your gazebo.

1 x 1-inch boards (panel keepers) are then nailed down the length of the 2 x 4 rails: on the bottom of the upper 2 x 4; along both the bottom and the top of the lower 2 x 4; and along the deck directly below those attached to the rails (see **Figure K**). The cedar panels and lattice panel can then be inserted, coming to rest against the 1 x 1-inch panel keepers. Two more 1 x 1-inch keepers are then installed outside each panel, securing them in place in both the upper and lower spaces.

Plexiglass or paned glass panels can be installed in much the same manner. One really nice idea is to build frames to which screen can be attached and inserted into the spaces. By making one side of the 1 x 1 panel keepers removable (use bolts and wing nuts instead of nailing in place) you can insert your screen panels in the summer and change over to glass for the winter.

The Bar

The bar is purely an option, but it is tremendously handy in keeping down the traffic at the doorway. Our bar replaces two latticework panels, which are boring things to build anyway.

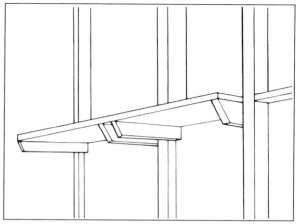

Figure O

The bar starts with braces made from 2 x 4-inch redwood, 18 inches in length (you can make the bar wider, longer, or shorter), and nailed to the sides of the posts between which the bar will rest (see **Figure O**). The braces extend under the 2 x 4-inch rail that separates the upper and lower panels so that the rail itself becomes part of the bar surface. 5½ inches of each brace extends beyond the rail into the interior of the gazebo while the remainder extends outward toward the great outdoors. The cedar paneling under the bar must be inletted to allow the braces to pass through.

As we said, the 2 x 4-inch rail forms one part of the bar surface, while another 2 x 4-inch board lies alongside, outside the post, extending the full length of the bar. On either side of these two boards are mounted two 2 x 6-inch boards that also run the full length of the bar. That's all there is – instant bar.

Finishing Up

The options available in building a gazebo party center are just the beginning. You may decide to install built-in seats, tables, and cabinets. You may wish to run water and electrical lines to your gazebo, or perhaps install a butane grill. You can literally add the kitchen sink if you so desire.

Get the whole family and maybe even a few friends involved in the planning and building. Tell them you're building a time machine to take them all back to the early 1900's, then ask them if they have ever heard of a "gazebo raising."

Options on the Gazebo Theme

Shown here are a few of the variations available to you. You'll note we said "a few," the gazebo design you will like the best is the one you think up yourself!

Illustrations A through D show options that can be incorporated without changing the basic structure as we have described it, only the wall panels are different. Illustration F shows our gazebo expanded to a 16 x 12-foot size requiring a slightly taller roof but maintaining the same roof slope.

We show a variation in floor plan and technique of laying decking in Illustration G. You'll note that the fire pit (if you choose to have one) can be positioned anywhere in the gazebo with a little forethought in floor joist placement.

A

GAZEBO PARTY CENTER

D

E

BUILDING OUTDOOR STRUCTURES

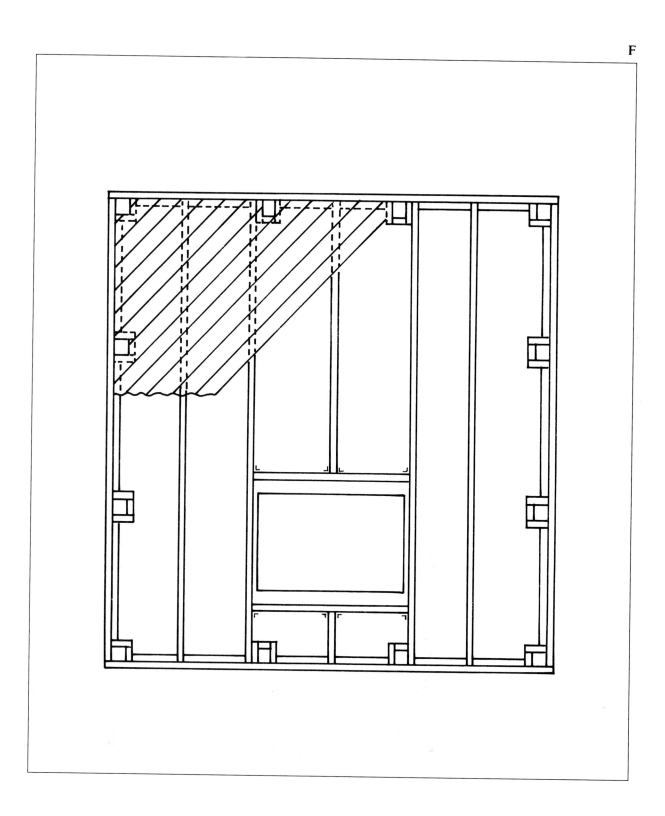

GAZEBO PARTY CENTER